Let praise and worship music lift you into God's presence.

For Christians eager for an understanding of the importance of praise and worship in our relationship with God, *Come and Worship* offers clear answers and scriptural guidance. The founders of Hosanna! Music write, "You can love the Lord and lead a good Christian life, but if you have never experienced the intimacy of expressing your feelings directly to God through the vehicle of music, you are missing one of the greatest joys of your own walk."

This insightful book not only instructs you in praising God; it also offers thrilling testimonies to the blessings received by those who continually offer up sacrifices of praise. You'll read of miraculous healings . . . victories against the forces of evil . . . hopelessly lost men and women surrendering their lives to Christ . . . and Christians rejoicing in times of tragedy . . . all because they reached out to God through praise and worship music.

Come and enter into deeper intimacy with God the Father.
Come and unleash the dynamic power of the Holy Spirit.
Come and adore Jesus Christ as never before.

Michael Coleman and Ed Lindquist invite you to *Come and Worship*.

COME
AND
WORSHIP

COME
AND
WORSHIP

MICHAEL COLEMAN & ED LINDQUIST

Published by
chosen books

FLEMING H. REVELL COMPANY
OLD TAPPAN, NEW JERSEY

First published, October, 1989
Second Edition, January, 1990

Library of Congress Cataloging in Publication Data

Coleman, Michael (Paul Michael)
  Come and worship / Michael Coleman and Ed Lindquist.
    p.   cm.
  Bibliography: p.
  ISBN 0-8007-9152-5
  1. Music in churches.   I. Lindquist, Ed.   II. Title.
ML3001.C69   1989   89-34590
264'.2—dc20   CIP
                                                                   MN

A Chosen Book
Copyright © 1989 by Michael Coleman and Ed Lindquist

Chosen Books are published by
Fleming H. Revell Company
Old Tappan, New Jersey
Printed in the United States of America

"A Mighty Fortress Is Our God," by Martin Luther (1483–1546). *Page 153.*

"Above All Else," by Kirk and Deby Dearman, © 1988 Integrity's Hosanna! Music. *Page 79.*

"Arise, My Soul, Arise," by Charles Wesley (1707–1788). *Page 149.*

"Be Still, My Soul," by Katharina von Schlegel (1697–?). *Pages 128–129.*

"Blessing, Glory, and Honor," by Clyde Holt, © 1978 His Eye Music/ Cherry Blossom Co. Adm. by The Sparrow Corp. *Page 148.*

"Boundless Love," by Richard Riley, © 1989, Integrity's Hosanna! Music. *Page 156.*

"Celebrate Jesus," by Gary Oliver, © 1988 Integrity's Hosanna! Music. *Page 138.*

"Come and Worship," by Don Moen, © 1988 Integrity's Hosanna! Music. *Page 136.*

"Come Into the Holy of Holies," by John Sellers, © 1984 Integrity's Hosanna! Music. *Page 83.*

"Crowned with Mercy" ("Bless the Lord"), by Bill McKenzie, © 1985 Integrity's Hosanna! Music. *Page 58.*

"For the Beauty of the Earth," by Folliott S. Pierpoint (1835–1917). *Page 137.*

"Go Forth," by Mark Altrogge, © 1987 People of Destiny Music. *Page 145.*

"God Is My Refuge," by Judy Horner Montemayer, © 1973 Integrity's Hosanna! Music. *Page 130.*

"Here in Your Presence," by Don Moen, © 1988 Integrity's Hosanna! Music. *Page 150.*

"Hosanna," by Gary Oliver, © 1988 Integrity's Hosanna! Music. *Page 142.*

"I Am the God That Healeth Thee," by Don Moen, © 1986 Integrity's Hosanna! Music. *Page 86.*

"I Hear Angels," by Gerrit Gustafson, © 1988 Integrity's Hosanna! Music. *Pages 26, 152.*

Acknowledgments

FIRST OF ALL, we want to acknowledge Diana Scimone's fine efforts. It was she who took all the teaching, testimonies, and stories about praise and worship from us and others, and put them down on paper. Without her long hours and hard work, this book would not have been done.

We want to thank Jane Campbell, editor of Chosen Books, who has been a supporter of our ministry from the beginning. After hearing about the testimonials that started to pour into our office from all over the world about what God was doing through praise and worship music, she encouraged us to share with others what we were seeing about this new move of God. Her resoluteness about getting us finally to sit down and start the project was most appreciated. So was the very capable assistance of Ann McMath, associate editor of Chosen Books, who helped us greatly with the editing process.

Very special thanks go to Elizabeth Sherrill; without her editorial ability, the book would have been far less readable and logical in its presentation. She really is the "best in the business" and we are most honored she agreed to help us out.

Finally, to the teachers, worship leaders, songwriters, Integrity Music staff, and our suppliers who have taught us

8

much and who have co-labored with us in getting praise and
worship music out to the nations: To these friends, our wives
and families, and to the many people who directly support our
organization by buying our products, and then openly share
with us their close encounters with God through praise and
worship music, this book is humbly dedicated.

May God's praises arise throughout the earth. Hosanna!

Michael Coleman

Ed Gundquist

Mobile, Alabama
Summer 1989

Contents

Introduction

HAVE YOU ever been white-water rafting? Then you know what it's like to start out in calm water, feeling pretty much in control. Soon, though, your raft enters the current; the wind hits you in the face, and the first set of rapids is upon you! Your adrenaline starts to flow, the guide calls orders, and you paddle as fast as your muscles will let you.

For the rest of the trip, you're swept along by a power greater than your own, at a speed and in a direction all its own. All you can do is hang on and enjoy the ride as your raft whirls you through rushing water and deep canyons into ever-widening vistas.

It's been four years since we founded Integrity Music. Our journey with our Guide during these exciting years has been a lot like a white-water raft trip. In the beginning, it seemed slow and easy and in full control, but it wasn't long before we realized we were being swept along by a powerful movement a lot bigger than we were—a "revolution" of praise that was sweeping the entire earth.

God has taken us into waters where we never expected to go. Why He called us and honored us to be a part of what He is doing today, we don't really know.

In 1984 we were both working for a Christian magazine published in Mobile, Alabama. At a staff meeting one morning that spring our circulation director announced the results of a recent survey to determine how we could better minister to our readers. His tabulation surprised everyone around the table.

"Just look at these figures!" he said. "Over and over again people are telling us they want more teaching on praise and worship."

When someone asked when was the last time we'd run an article on the subject, we checked the back issues file. "Looks like it's been a number of years."

To remedy this situation, we planned a series of articles about praise and worship. To us, it looked like a simple decision made in a routine editorial meeting. But it was more than that: Without our realizing it, God was leading us into uncharted waters.

Our first step was to locate someone who had a proven praise ministry, to share his expertise with the magazine audience. We contacted Terry Law, an evangelist based in Tulsa, Oklahoma, whose Living Sound music group had ministered in Poland, the Soviet Union, and other places normally closed to the Gospel. In August, September, and October 1984, we published three articles by Terry setting out the powerful principles he had learned about the place of praise and worship in spiritual warfare.

Our readers responded enthusiastically to the articles. Letters poured in, not only from this country, but from readers around the world whose lives were being changed by Terry's teaching. One man even wrote from Zimbabwe how God was revolutionizing his life as a result of reading the articles.

We were delighted by the tremendous response and wondered if there wasn't something more we could do in this area. But what?

In addition to the magazine, our ministry included a teaching tape program. Every month we'd send out a tape on a different subject of interest to Christians—prayer, perseverance, faith—featuring well-known Bible teachers. Over the years we'd developed a large and loyal audience; in fact, it was the largest and longest-running Christian tape program in the country.

Terry Law's teaching on praise and worship was powerful and met a need, but we began to see that people wanted praise and worship music itself. Our own lives had been changed in God's presence while worshiping Him, and in various churches and conferences both of us had seen for ourselves the power of music to lift worship onto a new plane. Now we wondered if our tape subscribers might be interested in receiving praise and worship music cassettes. We did another survey to find out, and the results were again very positive.

Though we'd had no experience in the music business, we did know something about running a tape program. Why not, we reasoned, combine this knowledge with the hunger that was so clearly out there?

Once again we wrote to our mailing list. This time we asked if people would be interested in a bimonthly praise and worship music tape—one they could "subscribe" to and receive in their mailbox every other month, just as they received the magazine and teaching tapes on a monthly basis.

The answer was overwhelmingly affirmative. Suddenly God had us poised at the edge of a new ministry. We took a deep breath and plunged in.

Our first task was coming up with the right songs for the tapes. We began to search for the best praise and worship songs anywhere in the Body of Christ regardless of denomination. We knew we wanted more than just "nice music." We were looking for music that would fulfill what we saw in the Scriptures—music that could actually bring people into God's presence where their lives could be changed.

Our first idea was to put together a "sampler" tape—the best songs from a variety of albums. But when we tried this approach, songs that sounded fine in their own context didn't flow together when placed side by side with very different pieces. Nor did they convey the excitement of a live worship service.

Our next idea was to find a suitable complete tape. Soon our offices were overflowing with cassettes—on the desks, stacked up on window sills, piled in boxes on the floor. But over and over again the same problem popped up. Tapes that had the right "spirit" didn't have professional audio quality. And the tapes that were recorded in studios on fancy equipment didn't have the feel of genuine live worship.

Just when it looked as if we had reached a dead-end before we even got started, God directed us to Tom Brooks. Tom lived in St. Louis and was producing tapes for the large church that he belonged to there. In February 1985 we heard one of his tapes and immediately sensed the presence of God in it. *And* it had the musical quality that we were looking for.

We knew this was the tape we wanted to send our subscribers as their first selection. In July 1985 we mailed this tape to 6,000 people all over the country.

It wasn't long before one of our customer service representatives came running into the office waving a piece of paper. It was the first letter about the new tape. And was it a good one!

> The tape arrived the day before we started vacation, which is what I was praying for. Can you picture a group of Christians gathering together in the great North Woods of Minnesota (Itaska State Park) and playing this

music to worship God? *Wow* and double *wow*! This
music has power. It draws you into praise and worship.
Thank you. And God bless you.

> Sincere love in Christ,
> Kathy Knuth
> Glencoe, Minnesota

Other letters followed. In fact, our mailroom, data opera-
tors, and customer service representatives could barely keep
up with the response. In letter after letter, people shared how
God had touched them while they were listening to the tape
and worshiping Him. It looked as if the tape was somehow
touching that deep hunger in the people of God to know Him
better.

We began to expand promotion of the music tape program
to other Christian mailing lists. In September 1985, we sent
our second tape to almost 10,000 people.

The response was so positive that we wondered if Tom
might be interested in working full-time with the ministry as
our producer. When we talked to him about it, we found that
God had already planted the desire in his heart—and in the
heart of his wife, Robin—to reach a wide audience with
quality, anointed praise and worship music. It was an answer
to prayer for all of us, and Tom has continued to work with us
as producer of these tapes.

And the Lord has continued to expand the ministry. In
1987 we formed a separate organization called Integrity Music
to focus exclusively on the praise and worship music ministry.
Today more than 175,000 people receive Hosanna! Music
Praise and Worship tapes every eight weeks.

Also in 1987, God opened the door for us to work with the
world's largest distributor of choral music, Alexandria
House, which has helped us take our best-known songs and

put them into octavo form for church choirs. September 1988 was another major opportunity for us when The Sparrow Company began distributing our tapes to Christian bookstores throughout the nation. And because we found this hunger is worldwide, we've set up ministry outreach centers in eight countries to distribute the tapes overseas.

We know a little more now about praise and worship music than when we first started, but we know too that our view is still through a glass dimly. Long before we sent out our first tape, we sensed that God was doing something very special through this kind of music—only we weren't sure of all that it involved. We began a search—a journey, if you will—to find out more. We prayed and we studied the Word of God. We talked with people all over the country and the world— ministers, teachers, worship leaders, and ordinary Christians who'd experienced revolutionary changes in their lives when they praised God in song. Out of that journey has come this book.

What we're discovering is that praise and worship music is having a profound impact on the Body of Christ. People are gaining a deeper relationship with the Lord, and unity is being restored throughout the Church. It encourages us to see churches across the nations coming together through this kind of music, regardless of religious background or denomination.

Two words of caution. First, in this book we'll be emphasizing praise and worship music because we believe it's something God is currently emphasizing. But it's only a *vehicle* into God's presence. In other words, don't worship worship. God is the focus of our worship. Praise doesn't heal; God heals. Worship doesn't mend broken relationships. Only God does.

Second, you can't use praise and worship to manipulate

God into blessing you. Your goal should be to bless Him and have a vital living relationship with Him. Praise and worship *music* is just one aspect of a praise and worship lifestyle. Music is the vehicle, but the goal is God's presence.

Do you want to be a part of this new wave of God? If your answer is "yes," this book is for you.

We'll show what happens when you come into God's presence, and outline specific steps to take you there. God is giving you an invitation—not just for a one-time experience, or even a once-a-week experience. He wants you to be in His presence constantly.

May God bless you as you join millions all over the world who are stepping into the throne room of the Father!

COME

AND

WORSHIP

1

Close Encounters

IT LOOKED like an ordinary bus, carrying just another group of young people. No one would have guessed the secret cargo hidden deep inside it.

To the outside observer, the passengers looked like young people anywhere. Some wore jeans, some were singing, others laughing. But this was no ordinary tour. These young people were actually musicians—Christian musicians traveling across Poland en route to the Soviet Union. Although the young evangelists had traveled to the U.S.S.R. many times before, this trip was particularly dangerous because in the cargo bins of the bus was a set of 24 master audiocassettes of the New Testament in Russian and three high-speed duplicators to copy the tapes and distribute them to underground Christians all over the Soviet Union.

For weeks before setting out, the group had prayed for wisdom on how best to hide the tapes and equipment to avoid detection by the border guards. The penalty for possessing duplicating equipment, or for trying to smuggle it into the Soviet Union, was an automatic ten years in prison. Finally the team had divided the tapes and duplicators into three packages, wrapped them in paper, spray-painted them black, and wedged the three parcels inside the case used for the transformers.

The plan seemed foolproof. But as the bus drove through the Polish countryside nearer and nearer to the border crossing, no one wanted to voice the apprehensions that were running through everyone's minds.

Fifty kilometers west of the border, Don Moen went to the front of the bus. Today creative director of Integrity Music, Don at that time was the leader of this group of young musicians. He began to lead the team in doing what they did best—worshiping the Lord. They sang every praise song they could think of—"We Bring the Sacrifice of Praise," "I Will Enter His Gates," "I Exalt Thee," and many others. For fifty kilometers, they lifted up the name of Jesus and sang about the power of His protection.

Finally the bus came to a stop at the Soviet border. Two stern-faced guards boarded the bus—an older man who seemed to be in charge, and a younger one who followed the other's lead. A third man, an interpreter, instructed some of the team to unload their personal belongings and take them into the customs house, while the others drove the bus to a separate area where they were directed to unload the sound equipment.

Nut by nut, bolt by bolt, and piece by piece, the two guards slowly worked their way through everything.

"Just keep calm," Don told the team quietly. "We've prayed, and God's in charge."

Don noticed that the older guard seemed to be losing interest in the search, but his assistant appeared more determined than ever to uncover something that would impress his superior with his thoroughness.

Oh, no, Don gasped to himself, *he's got the box of transformers where everything is hidden!* In a matter of seconds, Don realized, the guard would have the box untied, the paper removed—and the illegal tapes would be in plain view!

A shout from the older guard brought his heart to his mouth.

Don whipped around prepared to face the guard, but to his astonishment saw that the man was not yelling at him, but at his assistant. From his angry gestures Don surmised that he was bawling out the younger man for taking too long.

The assistant sheepishly set down the transformer case and went on to the other equipment, giving it only cursory inspection.

As he did so, the older guard strolled over to where Don was standing. "Please excuse him," he told Don through the interpreter. "He is new at his job and thinks he must be so thorough."

Completely astonished, Don and the team realized that a Soviet official was actually apologizing to them!

They also knew that this miracle at the border really began fifty kilometers west. As they praised and worshiped the Lord, the group had actually done battle with the enemy, "confounding" his script. Ephesians 2:2 calls Satan the "prince of the power of the air," indicating that he has actually set up his rulership in the heavenlies. As the team sang, their prayers and praises ascended to heaven, doing warfare in the spiritual realm. The result was that Satan's finely woven plans to expose their mission were totally unraveled at the border.

Although most of us seldom face such dramatic situations, we all encounter times when—like Don Moen—we need God's direct intervention: hopelessness, fear, anxiety, depression, sickness, even demonic opposition. The good news is that the power of God in everyday situations is just as real as it is in more exceptional ones. And one key to tapping into that power is praise and worship music.

In order to understand why this kind of music is so effective, we first have to define exactly what it is. Very simply, praise and worship music helps us experience the presence of God. There are seven elements that distinguish it from other types of Christian music.

One, it expresses praise, which the Bible tells us is the doorway to God's presence.

> Thou art holy,
>> O Thou who art enthroned upon the praises of Israel
>> [or "dost inhabit the praises of Israel"].
>>>> Psalm 22:3, NAS

> Enter his gates with thanksgiving
>> and his courts with praise.
>>>> Psalm 100:4

> Praise the Lord.
> How good it is to sing praises to our God,
>> how pleasant and fitting to praise him!
>>>> Psalm 147:1

> Praise the Lord.
> Sing to the Lord a new song,
>> his praise in the assembly of the saints.
>>>> Psalm 149:1

God invites us to come into His presence through praise. LaMar Boschman, who conducts seminars on praise and worship all over the country, puts it this way: If you were invited to meet the President of the United States, you'd be expected to enter his office in a certain way—in a respectful manner. Likewise when you meet the President of presidents, the King of kings, and Lord of lords, He invites you to come into His presence in a certain way: "Come rejoicing with music."

Two, praise and worship music is vertical. To oversimplify it, "horizontal" music talks *about* God, while "vertical" music talks *to* God. Horizontal music is directed from the musician toward another person, for exhorting, evangelizing, encouraging, or the like. Vertical music is directed from the musician upward to God. God is the audience and the believers are singing to Him. Both horizontal and vertical music are valid ministries; both have a place in the Church.

Three, praise and worship music can be sacrificial. Music is often called the voice of our emotions. If you're feeling good, you "whistle a happy tune." If you're feeling low, you "sing the blues."

But praise and worship music has nothing to do with our emotions or how we feel. That's why the Bible speaks of a "sacrifice of praise":

> Through Him then, let us continually offer up a sacrifice of praise to God, that is, the fruit of lips that give thanks to His name.
>
> Hebrews 13:15, NAS

Sometimes it's downright difficult to muster up anything that sounds like praise. Even spiritual giants have days when they can't find a thing to thank God for! Yet the Bible commands them—and us—to praise God *every* day, no matter how we feel, no matter what our circumstances: "Be joyful always; pray continually; give thanks in all circumstances; for this is God's will for you in Christ Jesus" (1 Thessalonians 5:16–18).

Four, praise and worship music is a "delivery system" for Scripture. This music "broadcasts" Scripture, internally to your spirit, and externally to attack the enemy—doubt, fear, or the devil himself. That's why many praise and worship songs are taken directly from the Bible. For example, the song "I Hear Angels" is based on Revelation 4–5, and 14:

I hear angels singing praises
I see men from every nation
Bowing down before the throne
Like the sound of many waters
Like a rushing wind around us
Multitudes join the song

And a symphony of praise arises
Tears are wiped away from eyes
As men from every tongue and tribe all sing
  Holy, holy God almighty
  Who was, who is and is to come
  All the angels are crying holy
  To the Lamb who sits upon the throne

Praise and worship music is a powerful way to help you proclaim Scripture, memorize it, and use it. It gives you an effective tool instantly at your disposal to oppose the works of the enemy.

Music is a powerful medium and, good or bad, once it's inside your mind, it tends to stay there. A recent survey in *U.S.A. Today* asked people if they could recall the lyrics to eighteen Beatles songs that were popular during the 1960s and 1970s. Surprisingly, even after twenty years, most people could remember more than 92 percent of the words.

Andrew Fletcher, an eighteenth-century Scottish patriot, once said, "If a man were permitted to make all the ballads, he need not care who should make the laws of a nation."

That's also why the devil has tried so hard to silence God's people from making music. In fact, for more than a century during the Middle Ages, congregational singing was forbidden in the churches. This ban was one of the practices that Martin Luther rebelled against during the Reformation. "Let God speak directly to His people through the Scriptures," he argued, "and let His people respond with grateful songs of praise." Luther responded, all right; he wrote 37 hymns, many still sung today.

Five, praise and worship music involves everyone. Danish theologian Soren Kierkegaard was critical of fellow Christians who never got involved in their churches' worship. He likened the church to a theater with prompters, players, and an audience. Many people, he pointed out, think that the musicians and choir are prompters, the ministers are the players, and the congregation is the audience. Instead, Kierkegaard declared, the church needs to change so that the musicians and ministers become the prompters, the congregation becomes the players, and God is the audience.

Because we live in a T.V. culture, we can get used to turning on a switch and being entertained. It's easy to expect this—even in church. But praising God isn't a "spectator sport." It's virtually impossible to be a worshiper and sit passively in a pew. That would be like a football player who spent the entire season sitting in the top row of the stadium watching his team play on the field below him. He might be technically part of the team, but he'd have no influence on the outcome of the game.

Six, praise and worship music springs from the heart. God is putting together a Kingdom of worshipers—not just in outward form, but in reality. Gerrit Gustafson, a member of the creative team for Hosanna! Music tapes, calls this Kingdom of worshipers an "international, transcultural, wholehearted, Spirit-filled community of reigning worshipers, in heaven and on earth."

Praise and worship music can't be an external act of mouth and lungs only; it has to be based on what's in the heart.

Jesus rebuked the silver-tongued Pharisees, questioning how such a "brood of vipers" could possibly speak anything good when their hearts were filled with hate: "For out of the overflow of the heart the mouth speaks" (Matthew 12:34).

Praise and worship music is an external expression of an

internal reality—a heart in love with Jesus, which leads us to our final point.

Seven, praise and worship music develops a praise and worship lifestyle. The Bible says that God is calling His people to become "true worshipers in spirit and in truth." How do we do this on a day-to-day basis?

The psalmist David did it through music. David was no super-pious holy man. He loved God, but sometimes he got angry. He served God, but sometimes he was rebellious. He felt the same hope, joy, fear, and frustration that we do. And he expressed them all in song to the Lord. Music was an integral part of David's walk with God.

You can love the Lord and lead a good Christian life, but if you have never experienced the intimacy of expressing your feelings directly to God through the vehicle of music, you are missing one of the greatest joys of your own walk.

God has created you for His pleasure, to bless Him. When you leave that area of your life empty—when you don't worship Him daily and give Him His rightful place in all that you do—it's very easy for other influences to make their way to the forefront—money, power, or any other idol.

God is issuing an invitation to His people—to you—to draw nearer. When Don Moen leads a worship service he often asks people to raise their hands if they sense God doing something new, drawing them into His presence in an unexplainable way. Just about everybody puts up a hand. Don then tells them they've experienced a "close encounter of the very best kind." Don wrote a song about the desire in every person's heart: "I Want to Be Where You Are":

> I just want to be where You are
> Dwelling daily in Your presence
> I don't want to worship from afar
> Draw me near to where You are

I just want to be where You are
In Your dwelling place forever
Take me to the place where You are
I just want to be with You

> I want to be where You are
> Dwelling in Your presence
> Feasting at Your table
> Surrounded by Your glory
> In Your presence
> That's where I always want to be
> I just want to be
> I just want to be with You

O my God, You are my strength and my
   song
And when I'm in Your presence
Though I'm weak, You're always strong

I just want to be where You are
In Your dwelling place forever
Take me to the place where You are
I just want to be
I just want to be with You
I just want to be
I just want to be with You

Don Moen and Gerrit Gustafson remember the time they
were giving a seminar on praise and worship in Jacksonville,
Florida. At the scheduled close of the session the presence of
God was so powerful that no one wanted to leave. Over and
over Don and Gerrit tried dismissing the meeting; it was
hours later before people reluctantly began to trickle out.

If all of us long for a "close encounter" with God, if His
presence is so satisfying that, once found, we want to linger
there forever, why is it that all people, all the time, don't
experience it? Let's look at four obstacles that get in our way

2

Four Roadblocks . . .
and How to Get Past Them

BETWEEN OUR own humanity and the ploys of Satan, there are many hindrances to our enjoyment of God's presence. The four most common are:
1) Failure to use the way He Himself has provided
2) A sense of unworthiness
3) A wrong image of who God is
4) Ups and downs of "feelings"
Let's look at them one by one.

1. We fail to realize that God the Father has made a way for us to come into His presence by His Son. In order to approach God's presence with a sincere heart, we must know that God wants us to come and fellowship with Him.

In the Old Testament Tabernacle, there was an outer court or the "holy place," and an inner court, or the "Holy of Holies." Between the two courts hung a thick veil or curtain representing the impassable gulf between God and man. In the Holy of Holies stood the Ark of the Covenant; into this inner court the high priest came once a year to offer blood for the sins of the people. Even he—the holiest man in Israel— was required to follow a strict regimen before entering God's presence, the place where God's shekinah glory dwelt:

> The Lord said to Moses: "Tell your brother Aaron not to come whenever he chooses into the Most Holy Place

behind the curtain in front of the atonement cover on the ark, or else he will die, because I appear in the cloud over the atonement cover."

Leviticus 16:2

The rest of the chapter lists detailed instructions about how Aaron was to prepare and cleanse himself before entering the Holy of Holies.

This Old Testament Tabernacle was a pattern or a shadow of the true Tabernacle in heaven, the very throne and presence of God Himself, and its symbolic structure was duplicated in the Temple that Solomon later built in Jerusalem.

Only the high priest, once a year, entered this innermost sanctum. Then . . . on the day Jesus was crucified, something unforeseen and unforeseeable occurred. Matthew 27:51 tells us that at the very moment of Jesus' death, the curtain in the Temple in Jerusalem that separated the holy place from the Holy of Holies was torn in two from the top to the bottom. The height and thickness of this veil made it impossible for any human being to tear it—and even if a human being had attempted to tear it, he would have attempted it from the bottom to the top. But God tore it from the top to the bottom to make it unmistakably clear that He Himself was doing away with the division between Himself and His people. Through the blood of Jesus He had made a way—the royal way, the only way—between Himself and humankind.

Therefore, brothers, since we have confidence to enter the Most Holy Place by the blood of Jesus, by a new and living way opened for us through the curtain, that is, his body, and since we have a great priest over the house of God, let us draw near to God with a sincere heart in full assurance of faith, having our hearts sprinkled to cleanse us from a guilty conscience and having our bodies washed with pure water.

Hebrews 10:19–22

God's invitation to us is evident in His gift of Jesus Christ, in that He gave His best—His only Son—as a sacrifice for our sin. The entire purpose of that sacrifice was to reconcile us to God and to give us fellowship with Him. But we must know that He did it—and why—before we can avail ourselves of the open door to His throne room. God has done it so that we can fellowship with Him. "God is faithful, through whom you were called into fellowship with His Son, Jesus Christ our Lord" (1 Corinthians 1:9, NAS).

2. *We are hindered from enjoying God's presence by a sense of guilt and condemnation.* "That all may be true," you may be saying, "but I could never be accepted by God because of the things I've done wrong." And you'd be right, of course, if your acceptance depended on your own performance. But it doesn't. Our acceptance depends on Christ's deeds, not ours.

> But because of his great love for us, God, who is rich in mercy, made us alive with Christ even when we were dead in transgressions—it is by grace you have been saved.
>
> Ephesians 2:4–5

The first thing that the Old Testament priests did when approaching the presence of God was to deal with their guilt. If we don't get past this point—and many people never do—we will never enter the Most Holy Place. Remember that our entire relationship with God is based on what He did for us at Calvary, not on anything we've done. Our salvation is based on His grace, not on our own works. In fact, there's nothing we could ever do that would make us righteous enough or holy enough to enter God's presence on our own merit! The Bible is very blunt about our personal righteousness before God: It is as "filthy rags" (Isaiah 64:6).

Christ's blood is the only thing that makes us righteous before God; it is this that has opened the new and living way into the Holy of Holies.

Jesus' righteousness is imputed to us on account of our faith in Him. It is a righteousness that cannot be shaken because it is God's own righteousness. If you do a good deed, it doesn't mean you're 85 percent righteous that day and can therefore come into God's presence. Or if you slam your hand in the car door and say something you shouldn't say, it doesn't mean that you're now only twenty percent righteous and excluded from communion with Him. First John 1:9 says if we confess our sins He cleanses us, making a way to restore our fellowship. But our reconciliation is not based on our works. God doesn't have a righteousness thermometer. You're either righteous or unrighteous, and the only way to be righteous before God is to believe in Christ's finished work on the cross.

In the Old Testament Tabernacle pattern, the blood of bulls and goats was offered as a sacrifice to cover sin and guilt. In Leviticus 17:11 the Lord told Moses,

> "For the life of a creature is in the blood, and I have given it to you to make atonement for yourselves on the altar; it is the blood that makes atonement for one's life."

The word *atonement* simply means "to cover." Hebrews 9:22 says, "Without the shedding of blood there is no forgiveness."

When the Israelites were slaves in Egypt God told them He was going to destroy all the firstborn in the land. In order to save their households from death He told them to select a Passover lamb, slaughter it, and dip a bunch of hyssop into the blood, putting some of it on the door frames of their houses. The death angel would not destroy anyone whose house was thus protected (Exodus 12:21–23).

Even so today the blood of Jesus—the spotless Passover Lamb—is over you, your family, and your house, and causes judgment to pass over you so that the destroyer cannot come near. Hebrews 10:22 declares you can draw near to God in complete faith because your heart has been "sprinkled to cleanse us from a guilty conscience and . . . our bodies washed with pure water."

What happened to the Israelites in the Old Testament has a New Testament application for you. The hyssop is your testimony. Revelations 12:11 says the saints "overcame him [Satan] by the blood of the Lamb and because of the word of their testimony, and they did not love their life even to death" (NAS).

Of course Satan does not want us to know this. He wants us to keep our eyes on ourselves, not on Jesus—to keep us mired in the sense of our own unworthiness. Revelation 12:10 calls Satan the accuser of the brethren, who accuses us before God "day and night." He's forever picking at our faults and weaknesses, attempting to discourage us from going on with God. He is unrelenting, heaping guilt and condemnation upon us to make us feel unfit for fellowship with God. But the Bible says there is a way to overcome Satan, and that is to testify to what the blood of Jesus has done for us.

Something almost miraculous happens when a Christian or group of Christians sings songs that testify to the power of the blood of Jesus Christ. His blood has brought about three changes in the fundamental nature of the believer.

First, Ephesians 1:7 says, "In him we have *redemption* through his blood." Redemption means that Christ has literally bought you and has taken control and ownership of your life. He has translated you out of the kingdom of darkness, the rule of Satan, and this world order, and He has brought you into His Kingdom, the Kingdom of God. His blood has purchased a new citizenship for you.

Second, Romans 5:9 says you have "been *justified* by his blood." Because of the blood of Jesus Christ you can say, "I am clean before God—just as if I'd never sinned." You have no basis to feel guilty in the Father's sight because there is no difference between Christ's righteousness and yours.

> Therefore, there is now no condemnation for those who are in Christ Jesus. . . . Who will bring any charge against those whom God has chosen? It is God who justifies.
>
> Romans 8:1, 33

Third, the blood of Jesus Christ *sanctifies* you and sets you apart as God's own to do His will. Through Christ's blood your human body becomes the sanctuary and dwelling place of God's own Spirit. Paul wrote to the church at Corinth, "Do you not know that your body is a temple of the Holy Spirit, who is in you, whom you have received from God?" (1 Corinthians 6:19).

Knowing the power of Jesus' blood—and that it has redeemed, justified, and sanctified you—gives you a basis for victory over the enemy and an ability to come before God without guilt or condemnation. This is why it's so important to sing songs about the blood.

> "Now have come the salvation and the power and the kingdom of our God, and the authority of his Christ. For the accuser of our brothers, who accuses them before

our God day and night, has been hurled down. They overcame him by the blood of the Lamb. . . ."

Revelation 12:10–11

3. We are hindered from enjoying God's presence by a false image of God. In Exodus 19, the people of Israel expressed a desire to be where God was. But as soon as they saw the "thick darkness" that surrounded God's presence—the thunder and the lightning—they became so frightened that they ran away. "From now on," they told Moses, "*you* go to God and tell us what He says. Don't let God come near us anymore lest we die." And the Bible says that from then on the people worshiped from afar.

Such fear comes from a misunderstanding of what God is really like. God is not unapproachable in His holiness, waiting to smite you with a swarm of locusts as soon as you make a mistake. Nor does He dangle your faults and weaknesses before you. In fact, Psalm 103:12 says that He has removed your transgressions as far from you as the east is from the west.

Just as the blood of Jesus supernaturally washes away your guilt, there is something that can supernaturally wash away your fear: God's love. The Bible says love is the antidote to fear: "There is no fear in love. But perfect love drives out fear" (1 John 4:18).

If you have a wrong image of God, it is because you have never realized how unconditionally He loves you. Perhaps your image of your heavenly Father is based on experiences with an earthly father who failed you. God will never fail you. He loves you and wants you to have fellowship with Him and to be comfortable in His presence. This was His plan from the beginning of time. He fellowshiped with Adam in the Garden, before sin ruptured the relationship. Jesus has made the way to restore it.

When we understand where fear comes from, we can deal

with it more effectively. Fear comes from Satan, not from God. There *is* a proper "fear" of the Lord, but it is clean and holy, based on an appropriate respect for God and for His power. It is not a cringing, cowardly kind of fear that would cause you to shrink back from His presence. Anytime you feel this negative kind of fear—an uneasiness and timidity that prevents you from approaching God—you can be sure it comes from the enemy. "For God did not give us a spirit of timidity, but a spirit of power, of love and of self-discipline" (2 Timothy 1:7).

Ask God for more of this stalwart spirit, and allow His love to heal any areas of fear.

4. We are hindered from enjoying God's presence by mood swings. Too often we tend to respond to God based on how we feel, rather than basing our faith in His Word and letting feelings follow. Praising God is often a "sacrifice of praise."

> Through Him then, let us continually offer up a sacrifice of praise to God, that is, the fruit of lips that give thanks to His name.
>
> Hebrews 13:15, NAS

A sacrifice of praise is a deliberate act of faith in God's Word, an outward manifestation of trust in Him—regardless of what is going on at the moment. Praise is a decision, an act of the will, not the emotions. Whether you've had a good day or a bad day doesn't really matter.

Let's say it's Wednesday evening about an hour before your Bible study meets. You've had a pretty good day. You've had the new neighbors to dinner. You helped one of your fellow employees through a difficult situation at work. And you agreed to head up a community blood drive. All in all, you're at peace with the world. That evening at the Bible study it's the easiest thing in the world for you to sing out the praise and worship songs heartily and to know you're entering God's presence.

Next Wednesday, however, things look different. The employee whom you helped at work steals from petty cash and your boss blames you. You chew out one of the kids at dinner unfairly. And you realize that the community blood drive is the same day as your daughter's tenth birthday party. Suddenly you're not feeling very spiritual. That night at the Bible study you mumble your way through the songs and God seems light years away.

He's not. He's right there—and He wants you and commands you to praise Him, even on the difficult days. If you do this—if you give thanks to His name, praise Him, and do it on a continuing basis regardless of what you feel—ultimately your feelings will line up with your words, and you will experience God's manifest presence.

Sometimes praising God will be a real battle. You'll have thoughts in your mind that will run directly contrary. Or there will be distractions around you while you try to concentrate on the Lord. You must deliberately move to focus your mind on God and His greatness, and off yourself and your circumstances.

The battle is for your mind and your thoughts. Have you ever been absorbed in something perfectly innocent when suddenly a wicked thought comes across your mind and you haven't the faintest idea where it came from? That's a fiery dart of the enemy. God wants to transform your thought life. Jesus said the first and greatest commandment was to "love the Lord your God with all your heart and with all your soul and with all your *mind*" (Matthew 22:37, emphasis added).

But the devil wants your thought life, too. He knows that if he can establish a beachhead in your mind, and then get your mouth to speak what's going on in your thoughts, he can begin to release his negative influences on your actions as well. There's power in what you confess. The mind is the center of the decision-making process, and the mouth is the voting box. What you say can determine what happens in the heavens and in the circumstances around you.

That's why offering praise to God on a daily basis is so critical. It's a major defense against the enemy's attacks. A heart filled with gratitude and a mouth that speaks gratitude will set up a powerful atmosphere around you as a spiritual barrier against Satan's spiritual ploys and tactics.

We can say, "I'm going to close out the enemy's words by trying *not to think* about them." But *not* admitting a thought is harder than assuming an offensive and positive stance— actively choosing to think about the Lord. Suppose the enemy presents you with a laundry list of all the reasons you shouldn't praise God in your current circumstances. If you believe Romans 8:28 that God causes all things to work together for good to those who love Him, you can begin then and there to praise God for allowing these circum- stances—and for the good He will eventually bring from them. We can spend so much time trying to change our circumstances that we never see that God wants to change us *in* our circumstances before He can deliver us *from* them. But if we can praise God in the midst of our circumstances, then the circumstances will no longer have control over us; we'll have the key to spiritual victory.

Terry Law knows all about praising God in the midst of devastating circumstances. In September 1982, Terry was in London for a board meeting of his music ministry when he received the news that his wife had been killed in a car accident.

Terry was shattered. He couldn't even pray, let alone praise; he became angry and bitter toward the Lord, blaming Him for letting his wife die.

"About three weeks after the funeral," Terry recalls, "my good friend Oral Roberts called me into his office. Oral had recently lost a son, and we talked for hours about the pain we felt. Finally Oral said he was going to share something that could save my life—my spiritual life. He told me to go home, get down on my knees, and start praising the Lord."

Terry thought Oral was crazy, but the next morning, as Terry relates in his book *The Power of Praise and Worship*, he got up early and tried to do what his friend suggested. "Immediately, the devil began to attack me, calling me a hypocrite," he says. "I was tempted to give up, but kept pressing through. Finally after two hours, I felt a pressure building up inside, like water behind a dam. Finally the dam exploded, and I began to weep and praise God all at the same time."

Terry learned firsthand about the "sacrifice of praise," a spiritual concept that has since shaped his entire ministry and helped him minister to thousands all over the world.

The Bible says, "The tongue has the power of life and death" (Proverbs 18:21). There's tremendous power—for good or bad—in what comes out of your mouth. When you praise God out loud with your lips, something happens in the heavenlies, as Paul and Silas discovered when they sang hymns in prison (Acts 16:25–26).

According to the Scriptures, a true New Testament sacrifice of praise is not silent. Now silence can be an acceptable position before God; there are times indeed when we're to be silent in His presence. But there are other times when we are to offer praise that is a verbal, out-loud expression of a heart in love with Jesus.

God the Father is seeking true worshipers. He is not

passively looking over the banister of heaven, but is actively looking for those who will respond to His invitation to come into His presence.

Remember that the blood of Jesus has forever dealt with your sin, your guilt, and your unworthiness. You have right standing with God—regardless of your self-evaluation, regardless of what kind of day you've had. Remember that God loves you, and His perfect love will cast out fear and correct misapprehensions about His character. And finally remember that there will be times when you'll have to thank the Lord and praise Him even when you don't feel like it. During those times you will be offering a true sacrifice of praise.

As Christians everywhere learn to overcome these hindrances to free communion with our Creator, we will see great victory in our personal lives, in our churches, and in the earth.

3

The Sound of His Presence

CHINA! The return address on the letter was from deep in the heart of this Communist stronghold. For the past several years, reports had filtered to the West about the widespread revival going on in the People's Republic of China. Now here was a letter from two missionaries sharing how God was using praise and worship music as part of this great move of the Spirit.

> Warmest greetings from our family in China! In Canada we came from an assembly where praise and worship was emphasized. Here in China few of the home churches know the truth of praise and worship. Your tapes really demonstrate to them the dynamics of worship. Even some unbelievers have borrowed the tapes. . . .

What is it about music that touches people everywhere? Not only across cultures but throughout the ages, praise music has brought people into a right relationship with God. In the Old Testament, music was an integral part of the worship of Jehovah. After Moses led the Israelites through the Red Sea, he led them in a song of praise to God for delivering them from the pursuing Egyptians: "I will sing to the Lord, for he is highly exalted. The horse and its rider he has hurled into the sea. The Lord is my strength and my song" (Exodus 15:1–2).

Later, during the time of Samuel, there was actually a school for prophets where students could learn—besides the Law and Hebrew history—psalms and music. The role of music in prophesying was vital: "As you approach the town, you will meet a procession of prophets coming down from the high place with lyres, tambourines, flutes and harps being played before them, and they will be prophesying" (1 Samuel 10:5).

Some people believe that David attended this school for prophets (see 1 Samuel 19:18). An accomplished musician himself, David knew how important it was to worship the Lord in music. When the Ark of the Covenant was brought up to Jerusalem, he appointed Asaph and a group of singers and musicians to go before it with songs of praise (1 Chronicles 15 and 16). Once the Ark was in place, he selected Levites "to minister before the ark of the Lord, to make petition, to give thanks, and to praise the Lord. . . . They were to play the lyres and harps, Asaph was to sound the cymbals, and Benaiah and Jahaziel the priests were to blow the trumpets regularly before the ark of the covenant of God" (1 Chronicles 16:4–6).

Then he taught them a psalm of thanks to the Lord: "Give thanks to the Lord, call on his name; make known among the nations what he has done. Sing to him, sing praise to him; tell of all his wonderful acts. . . . Sing to the Lord, all the earth" (1 Chronicles 16:8–9, 23).

Later David chose 288 of the sons of Asaph, Heman, and Jeduthun to minister with harps, lyres, and cymbals (see 1 Chronicles 25). These were musicians with a special prophetic anointing whose job was to offer songs of praise and worship to the Lord in the Temple. David also organized an enormous choir and orchestra of 4,000 Levites who were trained to be musicians before the Lord. He divided them into 24 groups so that they could play and sing before the Ark around the clock. David wrote much of the music that they played, and he passed on his songwriting skills to his son Solomon. When Solomon dedicated the Temple that he had built, he also appointed musicians and singers to minister to the Lord with trumpets and singing (2 Chronicles 5).

Praise and worship music continued to be an integral part of the reign of every one of Israel's godly rulers. When King Jehoshaphat was preparing to send an army against Ammon, Moab, and Mount Seir, such music was an integral part of his battle plan:

> Jehoshaphat appointed men to sing to the Lord and to praise him for the splendor of his holiness as they went out at the head of the army, saying: "Give thanks to the Lord, for his love endures forever." As they began to sing and praise, the Lord set ambushes against the men of Ammon and Moab and Mount Seir who were invading Judah, and they were defeated.
>
> 2 Chronicles 20:21–22

As the Israelites sang, the Lord set their enemies against one another until they were totally annihilated. It took Israel three days to carry home the vast amount of spoil left on the battlefield!

King Hezekiah restored the Levites, singers, and musicians to their proper place in the Temple ministering to the Lord (2 Chronicles 29–30). After the reign of the evil king Ammon, King Josiah cleansed the Temple and reappointed singers and musicians to worship God (2 Chronicles 35:1–19). During the reign of King Zerubbabel, among those returning to Israel after seventy years of captivity were "200 singing men and women."

> When the builders laid the foundation of the temple of
> the Lord, the priests in their vestments and with
> trumpets, and the Levites (the sons of Asaph) with
> cymbals, took their places to praise the Lord, as pre-
> scribed by David king of Israel. With praise and thanks-
> giving they sang to the Lord: "He is good; his love to
> Israel endures forever."
>
> Ezra 3:10–11

When Nehemiah finished rebuilding the walls of the city,
the dedication ceremony also included musicians and singers:

> At the dedication of the wall of Jerusalem, the Levites
> were sought out from where they lived and were brought
> to Jerusalem to celebrate joyfully the dedication with
> songs of thanksgiving and with the music of cymbals,
> harps and lyres. The singers also were brought together
> from the region around Jerusalem.
>
> Nehemiah 12:27–28

In more recent history, God has continued to use music to
draw His people near to Him. Judson Cornwall, who has
written a number of books on praise and worship (see
"Resources" on p. 155), observes, "Church history records
that any group that ruled out music as a part of worship had
a very short survival span." In fact, music has been part and
parcel of every revival in history.

It's easy to take for granted our easy access to Scripture,
teaching books, tapes, and other material important to our
Christian walk. But until 100 years ago, most people on earth
did not know how to read, and other media did not yet exist.
For centuries people depended upon the oral teaching of the
Church, including hymns, to disseminate the truth.

The Reformation in the sixteenth century placed as much emphasis on hymnwriting and singing as it did on preaching. Martin Luther was both a preacher and hymnwriter, using songs to underscore the messages that he proclaimed from the pulpit. John Calvin likewise wrote hymns in everyday language to tunes often taken from the folk music of the day. The great revivals of the eighteenth century led by men such as John and Charles Wesley and George Whitefield were carried throughout Europe and across to the United States by music. And in the nineteenth and twentieth centuries, revivals have always included both preaching and singing: preacher Dwight L. Moody and singer/songwriter Ira Sankey; Charles Finney and Thomas Hastings; Billy Graham and George Beverly Shea.

With the "Jesus Movement" that exploded in the mid-1960s, there was also an explosion of Christian music that combined elements from folk, country, Western, Southern, and hard and soft rock to come up with a style all its own.

In the late 1960s and early 1970s, God began to pour out His Holy Spirit all over the world. With this renewal of the Church came a fresh outpouring of praise and worship music, frequently taking Scriptures verbatim and setting them to music. Pioneering this type of music was Scripture in Song, a ministry based in New Zealand that is still very active today. Its leaders, David and Dale Garrett, have been instrumental in helping Christians all over the world come into God's presence by taking Bible verses and putting them to music.

All over the Body of Christ, people began to write songs of this kind. Some of them were professional songwriters, but many were not. They were housewives or construction workers or others with limited musical training. God would give them a song, which they'd sing in their local church. A visiting minister might hear it, and take it back to his own congregation. From there it would spread to yet another church. The process was repeated until some of these songs made their way clear around the world.

Today God is once again using music to draw His people closer to Him. It's happening all over the earth, across denominational lines, across age groups, across cultural barriers.

And wherever it happens, a special and marvelous anointing follows. . . .

From the beginning of our ministry, we've always put an emphasis on prayer to seek God's direction and help for all that we do. One particular morning, about a year or so after we mailed our first tape, God gave us a specific word from Isaiah 61 that became the mission statement for our ministry:

> The Spirit of the Sovereign Lord is on me, because the Lord has anointed me to preach good news to the poor. He has sent me to bind up the brokenhearted, to proclaim freedom for the captives and release for the prisoners, to proclaim the year of the Lord's favor and the day of vengeance of our God, to comfort all who mourn, and provide for those who grieve in Zion—to bestow on them a crown of beauty instead of ashes, the oil of gladness instead of mourning, and a garment of praise instead of a spirit of despair . . . For as the soil makes the sprout come up and a garden causes seeds to grow, so the Sovereign Lord will make righteousness and praise spring up before all nations.
>
> verses 1–3, 11

We knew this was a prophetic passage—a Messianic passage—describing what Jesus' ministry would be when He appeared in human flesh. Many centuries after these words were written, Jesus read them aloud in the synagogue at Nazareth, declaring, "Today this scripture is fulfilled in your hearing" (Luke 4:21).

There are many glorious truths in these verses from Isaiah, but the ones that came alive to us during our time of prayer related to the results of God's anointing on Jesus. We saw that it was the Spirit of the Lord upon Jesus who inaugurated His ministry. But there was even more: The passage as a whole is about the restoration of God's people that would occur because of Christ's coming. The same Spirit who rested on Jesus Christ rests on those who are His. And because this is true, the same kind of ministry can flow through us.

Next we looked at the operative or "action" words in these verses, and saw that God's restored people are empowered to preach, to bind, to proclaim, to comfort, to provide. But the action word that seemed to leap from the page at us all was *bestow:* "to bestow on them a crown of beauty instead of ashes, the oil of gladness instead of mourning, and a garment of praise instead of a spirit of despair" (verse 3).

What struck us so vividly is that there is a ministry or anointing of the Holy Spirit on God's people that actually allows them to bestow on those who mourn and who despair a garment of praise and the oil of gladness! A garment of praise, or as some translations call it, a "mantle," is like a cloak or something that you wear, and it will overcome a spirit of despair. We began to see that there is a ministry that God gives His people of granting and encouraging—a garment of praise and the oil of gladness—that is different from the other ministries of the Spirit listed in verses 1 and 2.

Finally we saw something very special in verse 11: "For as the soil makes the sprout come up and a garden causes seeds to grow, so the Sovereign Lord will make righteousness and praise spring up before all nations."

God Himself will cause righteousness and praise to spring up! We rejoiced when we read this because we realized that through the medium of music we were a part of His great work of encouraging people all over the earth to praise Him.

As we continued praying and studying the Scriptures, we realized that drawing close to God through praise and worship music, and spending time in His presence, would release these additional ministries of the Holy Spirit to His people. There would be anointing . . .

"To preach good news to the poor"—evangelism;

"To bind up the brokenhearted and comfort all who mourn"—inner healing;

"To proclaim freedom for the captives and release for the prisoners"—deliverance;

"To proclaim recovery of sight for the blind"—physical healing;

"To proclaim the year of the Lord's favor and the day of vengeance of our God"—God's favor and judgment;

"To provide for those who grieve in Zion"—gladness and hope.

This Scripture passage also suggests that as we spend time in God's presence in praise and worship, and as more and more people all over the world do this, His wonder-working power will be manifested increasingly through "ordinary" men and women.

4

Receiving God's Power

"The Lord has anointed me."
Isaiah 61:1

MARY JANE KEPPLER had packed carefully for the
long-awaited retreat—a camera, rolls of extra film, a
Bible, a tape recorder, and a copy of a praise and worship
tape she'd just received, "All Hail King Jesus." She and her
sister had traveled from Strawberry Point, Iowa, to the site of
the retreat, Medjugorje, Yugoslavia. Here, the Lord told
Mary Jane, He was going to use her like Moses to "stand in
the gap" for others.

So as soon as Mary Jane and her sister got settled in their
hotel room in Yugoslavia, they began to pray for the other 36
members of the tour group, many of whom they had only just
met. They asked God to send anyone with a special need
directly to them.

They hadn't even finished praying when there was a knock
on the door. Two ladies from the group were standing there,
one of them clearly in extreme pain. "Would you pray for my
back?" she asked.

Mary Jane invited them in, put her tape into the player, and
the four began to praise and worship God along with the music.
Then Mary Jane and her sister placed their hands on the
woman's back and prayed that God would send healing to it.

"I feel something!" she cried after a few minutes. "It feels all warm and tingly!" Soon every trace of pain had disappeared.

God continued to work through Mary Jane and her sister. They invited other members of the group to their tiny room; together they prayed and sang and praised God. "The presence of the Lord was so strong," Mary Jane recalls, "that one by one each of the newcomers was filled with the Holy Spirit."

Is there something special about Mary Jane? She would be the first to answer no! The anointing of the Lord is for *all* who believe.

The word *anointing* literally means to "pour, smear, or rub over with oil." It's used in the Old Testament to describe the consecration of a person to God's service, and symbolizes the Spirit of the Lord coming upon him to enable him to fulfill his call. Recall, for example, what Samuel did when he selected David from among his brothers to become king: "So Samuel took the horn of oil and anointed him in the presence of his brothers, and from that day on the Spirit of the Lord came upon David in power" (1 Samuel 16:13).

The same procedure was followed in the consecration of priests. Exodus 29 gives detailed instructions for the setting apart of Aaron, concluding: "Take the anointing oil and anoint him by pouring it on his head" (verse 7).

Leviticus 8 shows that objects as well as persons could be dedicated to God's service in this way:

> Then Moses took the anointing oil and anointed the tabernacle and everything in it, and so consecrated them. He sprinkled some of the oil on the altar seven times, anointing the altar and all its utensils and the basin with its stand, to consecrate them. He poured

some of the anointing oil on Aaron's head and anointed
him to consecrate him.

verses 10–12

Psalm 133 refers to this "precious oil" that was poured on
Aaron's head, comparing it to the dew that falls on Mount
Zion, "for there the Lord bestows his blessing, even life
forevermore" (verses 2–3).

In the New Testament there's a radical expansion of this
concept of priesthood. No longer reserved for a particular
bloodline in a particular place, *all* who trust in Jesus' finished
work on the cross, whoever we are, wherever we are, are
anointed for God's service. "But you are a chosen people, a
royal priesthood, a holy nation, a people belonging to God,
that you may declare the praises of him who called you out of
darkness into his wonderful light" (1 Peter 2:9–10).

Our anointing comes from the same Spirit who empowered
the kings and priests of ancient Israel, the same Spirit who
was with God in the beginning, the same Spirit who raised
Jesus from the dead. Because of Jesus' death and resurrection,
this third Person of the Trinity dwells today in your mortal
body! "Do you not know that your body is a temple of the
Holy Spirit, who is in you, whom you have received from
God?" (1 Corinthians 6:19). And it is this indwelling Spirit
who will perform the work He calls you to do. As Bible
teacher Ern Baxter has described it, the Father thinks it, the
Son speaks it, and the Holy Spirit does it. He is the executive
agent of the Godhead.

In four essential areas, the activities of the Holy Spirit are
the same for each one of us.

1. The Holy Spirit exalts Christ. Jesus told His disciples,
"He will testify about me" (John 15:26) and "He will bring
glory to me" (John 16:14). Later Paul wrote to the church at

Corinth: "Therefore I tell you that no one who is speaking by the Spirit of God says, 'Jesus be cursed,' and no one can say, 'Jesus is Lord,' except by the Holy Spirit" (1 Corinthians 12:3).

2. The Holy Spirit reveals our sinfulness. "When he comes, he will convict the world of guilt in regard to sin and righteousness and judgment" (John 16:8).

3. The Holy Spirit provides guidance. "It is for your good that I am going away. Unless I go away, the Counselor will not come to you; but if I go, I will send him to you" (John 16:7).

4. The Holy Spirit shows us the truth. Jesus promised, "But when he, the Spirit of truth, comes, he will guide you into all truth . . . and he will tell you what is yet to come" (John 16:13).

"And it is the Spirit who testifies, because the Spirit is the truth" (1 John 5:6). When you proclaim the truth, whether in testimony, preaching, or song, the Holy Spirit bears witness and affirms it.

> This salvation, which was first announced by the Lord, was confirmed to us by those who heard him. God also testified to it by signs, wonders and various miracles, and gifts of the Holy Spirit distributed according to his will.
>
> Hebrews 2:3–4

One way God shows us His truth is through signs and wonders; He manifests Himself so that you can say, "Amen! That's God!" God always confirms Himself. This is the reason for the miraculous testimonies throughout this book. Everything the Holy Spirit says and does is designed to draw people to Jesus—including the praise revolution that is growing today.

"That's fine," you might say, "but I'm no Paul, or Peter, or John. I'm just *not* a spiritual powerhouse!"

When you worship God, you have at your disposal the very same Spirit that Paul, Peter, and John tapped into—the Holy Spirit. And He will anoint you—just as He anointed them—to preach, to heal, to evangelize, and so forth. In the Old Testament, priests were born into the tribe of Levi, but could not perform as priests until they were anointed. You, too, are a priest—a New Testament priest to minister to God—and you've already been anointed by the Holy Spirit Himself:

> You are a chosen race, a royal priesthood, a holy nation,
> a people for God's own possession, that you may pro-
> claim the excellencies of Him who has called you out of
> darkness into His marvelous light.
>
> 1 Peter 2:9–10, NAS

The Hebrew word *kohen*, translated into English as "priest," literally means "one who draws near to the divine Presence." How do we draw near to the divine Presence? Through worship! "He has made us to be a *kingdom, priests* to His God and Father" (Revelations 1:6, NAS, emphasis added).

Jack Hayford, pastor of Church on the Way in Van Nuys, California, and author of many songs, believes that worship is at the very heart of God's program for restoring man's dominion. "Our role as worshiping priests," Jack writes in his book *Worship His Majesty*, "is the means to our role as reigning kings. . . . Our dominion *in* Him is directly corre-lated to our worship *of* Him."

But the specific ministry to which such worship will lead

will be as unique as each individual. Dolly Holland of Hurricane, West Virginia, for example, works with Hurting Women's Ministry, reaching out to needy women of all descriptions. Dolly has found that when she praises God— even just by playing praise tapes in her office as she works— she is ready to confront the heartbreaking problems that come through her door. She can do it because as part of the "royal priesthood," she is extending the Lord's rulership to the world that she touches on a daily basis.

George Hobson watched worship equip a young man for evangelism. At the Bible college that George attended in Baton Rouge, Louisiana, an outreach group called the "Soul Patrol" planned to go to New Orleans during the city's 1988 Mardi Gras festivities. With its strong bent toward the occult, Mardi Gras for most people is an excuse for immoral excesses. The Soul Patrol knew that this was a prime spot to share the truth about Jesus.

Anticipating spiritual warfare, George shared some of his praise and worship music tapes with the young men on the team. One of these students was what George calls a "reserved intellectual," but as they worshiped God with the music on the tape, George saw his friend change into "a man I'd never seen before." The usually introverted and self-conscious young man began to praise God with joy and freedom as the presence of God came down upon him, giving him a special anointing that lasted through many days of effective witnessing in New Orleans.

Anna Scheller, who lives with her husband on Laughlin Air Force Base in Texas, also planned to go to New Orleans to evangelize during Mardi Gras. "It was my first time street witnessing ever," she recalls, "and I was very apprehensive. Often I questioned whether God was really calling me to do this." As she and her husband drove to the airport, they played a praise and worship tape, "Steadfast Love." Suddenly Anna realized that God was using one song on the tape "The Name of the Lord," from Proverbs 18, to speak to her about her trip:

> O the name of the Lord
> It's like a strong tower
> The righteous shall run to it
> And be glad
>
> Then they'll go forth in victory
> Triumphing over the enemy
> Yes, they'll go forth
> To kick in the gates of hell
> For they are the army of God
> For they are the army of God

Anna knew that God was telling her she was a part of His army going to New Orleans to "kick in the gates of hell," and that He would give her the anointing she'd need to carry out His mission. "He showed me I didn't have to be afraid because His name was my strong tower. I started to get excited about what was going to happen!"

God didn't let Anna down. In her suitcase Anna had packed the puppets that she uses to minister God's love to children. She and another Christian from Minnesota spent their time in New Orleans entertaining children who were waiting for the Mardi Gras parades to pass by, seeing a number of them accept Jesus into their hearts.

A family in Poland received a very different anointing while they were praising God in song. For some time, they had been seeking God for the answer to a crucial question: Should they try to emigrate to West Germany, or stay behind the Iron Curtain to work for the Lord? As they were worshiping God in song, they felt Him tell them two things: One, they should stay in Poland, and two, He would supply the strength they'd need to carry on the work He would call them to do.

Recently they wrote a letter telling about their difficult decision. "It is not so easy to live in our country," they said, "but now we're sure that with Him we can live and do whatever must be done."

Power to venture forth. Power to stay put. Power to minister to the hurting. None of it is our own; all of it flows from the anointing of God on His priests as He consecrates each of us to His service. Let's look now at the various forms this anointing can take.

5

Power to Evangelize

"To preach good news to the poor."
Isaiah 61:1

MARK GARFIELD (not his real name) was an empty, rebellious man without any real purpose or meaning in his life. His wife and three children had prayed for him for years, but his aimless, godless existence finally got the best of him, and Mark committed a crime that put him behind bars at a correctional facility in South Carolina.

While Mark was in jail, someone gave him a praise and worship music tape, "In His Presence." Words such as these from the song "Crowned with Mercy," from Psalm 103, touched Mark deep inside:

> O bless the Lord, O my soul
> And all that is within me
> Bless His holy name
> Forget not all His benefits
> For He's forgiven you
> And sent His Word to heal you
>
> O bless the Lord, O my soul
> And all that is within me
> Bless His holy name
> Remember all His love for you
> For He's redeemed your life from death
> And crowned you with mercy

Right there in his cell, Mark got down on his knees and asked God to forgive his sins and make his life new again

Today Mark does indeed have a new life. He has a new relationship with his wife, children, and parents, and regularly attends church services in prison while he's waiting to be released.

Mark's story illustrates how the Holy Spirit convicts of sin and brings people to Christ. This is God's presence bringing "good news to the poor," and it happens when unbelievers are brought into an atmosphere of praise and worship.

At first glance, it might not seem that worship and evangelism go hand in hand. After all, worship is directed to *God*, while evangelism is directed to *people*. How could one influence the other? Yet David sang, "He put a new song in my mouth, a hymn of praise to our God. Many will see and fear, and put their trust in the Lord" (Psalm 40:3).

The spiritual principle operating here is one mentioned earlier: God inhabits the praises of His people. When we praise Him, we give the Holy Spirit "living room." And as John 16:8 says, one of the Holy Spirit's ministries is to bring people to repentance and draw them to Jesus.

Dwight L. Moody, the nineteenth-century American evangelist, observed, "Singing does at least as much as preaching to impress the Word of God upon people's minds. Ever since God first called me, the importance of praise expressed in song has grown upon me."

The reason that singing praise songs to the Lord is so powerful is the same reason that preaching is so powerful: In both cases people are hearing truths of God proclaimed. And that can result in repentance and salvation. Robert Williams of Mobile, Alabama, knows exactly what that means. Rob accepted Jesus as his Savior when he was four years old, but spent forty years running away from God. The last thing he wanted was a personal relationship with the Lord. Nor did he feel comfortable around those "Jesus people"—all they ever did was talk about Jesus, all the time!

Then Rob's company gave him a new sales territory in a rural area, and he found himself spending long hours in his car between service calls. One morning as he was leaving for work, his wife, Carol, gave him a tape to listen to as he drove. Rob looked at the title: "Give Thanks." *It's Christian music,* he groaned to himself, and tossed the tape into his briefcase.

Later that day he decided to give the tape a try, but after just a few songs, the tape landed back in his briefcase. *All that Jesus music sounds alike!* he said to himself.

Yet Rob couldn't stop thinking about what he had heard. After a few miles, he pulled the tape out and played it again—and again, and again, and again. The anointing of the Holy Spirit so overwhelmed him with blinding tears that he had to pull off the road. There God reached down and gently drew Rob Williams back into His fold.

There are many promises in the Bible that foretell the kind of thing that happened to Rob in Alabama and Mark in South Carolina. Psalm 102, for example, says:

> The nations will fear the name of the Lord, all the kings of the earth will revere your glory. . . . Let this be written for a future generation, that a people not yet created may praise the Lord.
>
> verses 15, 18

In England, singer/songwriter Graham Kendrick is seeing this Scripture promise come to life. Graham heads a ministry called Make Way Music that organizes praise marches all over the country. At the City March in London in 1987, 15,000 enthusiastic Christians came out in the pouring rain to sing, dance, play instruments, and praise God as they marched through the streets of the city. The next year a crowd of 60,000 from a host of different Christian denominations turned out. Now Christians all over the United Kingdom are making plans for a giant nationwide "March for Jesus" that will involve more than half a million people. From John O'Groats on the northern tip of Scotland to Land's End on the southern tip of England, marchers will be linked by satellite and telephone as they take to the streets simultaneously to praise God.

"We need to grasp the present opportunity to establish a prophetic voice in the affairs of our nation," says Graham. He envisions "a prophetic presence on the streets" leading to "a massive spiritual revival, while reintroducing people to the church as a joyful company of ordinary people, full of life and color." Graham says there are four reasons why praising God before nonbelievers can result in repentance and salvation.

1. Praise sets forth the truths of God's Kingdom. Whether in a church setting or out on a public street, praise and worship are powerful tools because they declare the nature of God, and extol the power of His Word and Jesus' blood. "In our Make Way marches," Graham explains, "we've seen the Spirit of God touch people as the marchers have gone past. They'll break down in tears and be led to the Lord simply because the Spirit of God is present in the praises of His people."

Graham stresses the importance of maintaining a balance between praise and preaching in reaching out to non-believers. Both, he says, are necessary. As we worship before them, "nonbelievers may feel the presence of God come upon them, but they've still got to have someone explain the Gospel to them." One London group that has organized many citywide marches noticed that when they followed their marches with more traditional evangelism—preaching, one-to-one witnessing, leaflet distribution, drama teams, and so on—they saw much higher rates of conversion than with the marches alone.

2. *Praising God in public places—either with marches, with singing, or by simply playing a praise and worship tape on a cassette player—gives the Church a visible, physical presence.* Most nonbelievers think of "church" as something that goes on behind closed doors—something boring and unconnected to everyday life. But once they see people celebrating and actually *enjoying* God, they want to know where this joy comes from.

Graham says that on more than one occasion he has heard people comment, "If I thought church was really like that, I'd seriously think about going." He adds that the day of Pentecost is a prime example of a worshiping church that affected nonbelievers around it. They saw something remarkable happening there in the streets before their eyes, and they asked, "What must we do to be saved?"

A good example of this particular anointing is what happened to Bob Mason. Bob is a singer and author as well as associate pastor at Church on the Rock near Dallas, Texas, pastored by Larry Lea and Lawrence Kennedy. A few years ago Bob was with a singing group, "Living Praise," ministering in a large Southern city during an annual celebration. Living Praise had prayed and fasted for weeks to prepare for the time of ministry, and Bob was confident that the group's musical abilities could attract and hold a crowd.

In fact, 3,000 people at a time gathered in a park to listen to the group, but the moment the songs were over and the musicians would start to share the Gospel, their listeners would melt away.

"God," Bob prayed, "how can we get through to these people?"

"Don't sing *about* Me," the Lord answered him. "Sing *to* Me. Just worship Me."

Bob felt a little foolish, but closing his eyes so that he couldn't see anyone, he lifted his hands and began to worship the Lord.

When he opened his eyes, he saw that the people were staring, seemingly rooted to the spot. Bob's group just continued worshiping God, singing and dancing around the stage as they lifted up His name. And the Holy Spirit began to move. Almost 2,000 people were born again during the five days that the group ministered.

3. *When we praise God in the presence of nonbelievers, we engage in spiritual warfare.* Praise clears the spiritual atmosphere, Graham says, and removes the spiritual blinders that prevent people from seeing the Lord. There is a sequel to Bob Mason's story that illustrates this point. A few months after that particular time of ministry, Bob was talking to a friend of his who pastors a church there. The pastor told Bob about a man who had come to the church with deep spiritual problems—in fact, with every evidence that the devil had a firm grip on this man. Through prayer, counseling, and deliverance, the man was set free and became a Christian. Several weeks later, the man overheard some tapes at a picnic. He went over to ask the name of the group doing the singing. "Living Praise," he was told.

"I knew it!" he exclaimed. "I recognized that spirit."

He explained that he had been a member of a coven, or satanic church, for ten years. His "ministry" was to travel around the country and sit in churches beaming "fiery darts" at the pastors. He would project lewd thoughts toward their minds, or will confusion so that they would become lost in their sermons.

Earlier that year, he went on, he had been in a certain city with his coven. As they had neared the park where Living Praise was singing, a demon spoke very clearly to him: "Do not go near them! Turn right now and run in the other direction. Don't even get close to those people. Run as fast as you can. Don't have any contact with them, and don't get within earshot of their music."

But it was too late; the man could clearly hear the music. Furthermore, he realized that the devil could not be the ultimate power because obviously there was something the devil feared. When the man next went to a church he found he could not disrupt the pastor. He knew further that something was happening to him when he heard the praise and worship. Because of that experience, he was saved and delivered of the stranglehold that the devil had on him.

4. *And, finally, nonbelievers are drawn to the Lord when they witness our unity.* Jesus prayed "that all of them may be one, Father, just as you are in me and I am in you . . . that the world may believe that you have sent me" (John 17:21).

When we stand publicly with other Christians to declare the Lordship of Jesus, there is a power released that touches people. When Graham organizes a Make Way march, he tries to include as many Christian churches in each city as possible. "Each church carries a banner with its name on it," he says. "Baptists, Methodists, Pentecostals, Anglicans—everybody's represented. Bystanders look at the banners and say, 'Good grief! They're *all* out there!' "

Nonbelievers all over the world are coming to know Jesus as His followers worship Him. In Randburg, South Africa, Dudley and Margie Reed have been leading worship seminars for many years. Recently Dudley formed a team of young people who were willing to commit a year of their lives to evangelism. On the team's first outreach, they visited tribal villages in a remote area of the country and led more than 400 people to the Lord. The chief of one village received Jesus and was healed of bad eyesight; in another, the local witch doctor accepted Jesus as his Lord and Savior, and was water-baptized. All this happens, the Reeds say, as God's people give themselves in worship.

Queensway Cathedral in Toronto, Canada, armed their ministry teams with praise and worship tapes when they visited churches in Uganda. Explains Tom Morris, missions pastor: "I took two tapes to Kampala, the capital, on a recent trip and donated them to Gary Skinner, a missionary based there. He used them with his singing group, Incense, and it's resulted in a strengthening of their ministry. By nothing short of a miracle, we were allowed to minister in the world's third-largest prison just outside Kampala. The 8,000 inmates who wear nothing but rags and sleep on reed mats heard this music and listened to us as we preached the Word of God. Eighty percent responded to the message and raised their hands to accept Jesus as their Lord. This is indeed 'good news preached to the poor'!

"I wish you could see the youth choir in Kampala sing 'Blessing, Glory, and Honor,' " Tom Morris adds. "The building where they meet was once a torture chamber for Idi Amin. There is still blood staining the walls from those days. Now it is the largest church in Uganda. Truly our God is honored by worship."

The book of Revelation states that Jesus' sacrifice purchased men from every tribe and tongue:

"You were slain, and with your blood you purchased men for God from every tribe and language and people and nation. You have made them to be a kingdom and priests to serve our God, and they will reign on the earth."
Revelation 5:9–10

This Scripture has particular meaning for Eugene Thompson, an Ojibwa Indian who lives on Lac Court Oreilles Indian Reservation in Hayward, Wisconsin. Most Indians there are pagans. Eugene himself once drummed and sang at pow-wows. But with a handful of other Indians he now sings a new song.

The fledgling church first met in a two-car garage, then in a building off the reservation. Now they have their own trailer where they meet to praise God in words and music. Sometimes the temperature in the trailer plunges to fifty degrees below zero. Other times it is blisteringly hot and full of mosquitoes. But the Lord is moving through the worship of these faithful people.

"It's very hard to stop hearing the drums from our old Indian ways," says Jane Mitchell, Eugene's cousin. "I suppose you'd have to see to believe how proud Indian people are of their heritage. But now a handful, including me, are re-learning our real heritage."

Far away in the Philippines, people are also being touched by praise and worship music. Missionaries Gerald and Donna Johnson and their "Good News Praise and Worship Team" recently held a crusade on the island of Mindanao. It took them two days to travel up the mountains to the crusade site, but they were rewarded with 467 people who prayed the sinner's prayer during the ten-day crusade. Today there is a thriving church in that remote village.

> "And I . . . am about to come and gather all nations and tongues, and they will come and see my glory. I will set a sign among them, and I will send some of those who survive to the nations—to Tarshish, to the Libyans . . . to Tubal and Greece, and to the distant islands that have not heard of my fame or seen my glory. They will proclaim my glory among the nations."
>
> Isaiah 66:18–19

6

Power for Inner Healing

"To bind up the brokenhearted" and "comfort all who mourn."

Isaiah 61:1

FOR JOANN CARLUCCI (not her real name) life seemed hopeless. Her husband had deserted her, taking their two-year-old son. She lost first her job, then her car, then her apartment. At her lowest point, she started believing the lies that the devil threw at her—that she was responsible for being sexually molested as a young girl, that she was to blame for her father's suicide. In her own eyes, her life was so utterly worthless that death seemed a less painful alternative.

Then a friend gave JoAnn some praise and worship tapes. In her loneliness she played and replayed them. Gradually the Scripture words on the tapes began to "reprogram" her mind from negative thoughts to positive hope. Over and over again she played the tapes, until the Word of God was planted in her heart and mind. Slowly God began to heal her from the inside out, washing her of hurts she'd carried for years.

JoAnn now has a new job, is feeling better physically than she's felt in years, and is on the road to being debt-free. As 2 Corinthians 5:17 promises, she is a "new creation; the old has gone, the new has come!"

"Inner healing," or healing of the brokenness and grief that we carry inside, is another of the tremendous rewards that can come about when we enter God's presence. Perhaps you've been unable to stop grieving for the loss of a loved one. Maybe you were abused as a child and that need for inner healing is poisoning your relationship with your spouse. Perhaps your parents divorced when you were young and you've felt rejected ever since.

No matter what the inner wound, the antidote is the same. You need the healing and the hope that only God can provide.

Our God is the God of hope. He's in the business of restoring our vision of the future. These are the words that Isaiah used to describe the ministry of the Messiah 700 years before Jesus was born: "He will not shout or cry out, or raise his voice in the streets. A bruised reed he will not break, and a smoldering wick he will not snuff out" (Isaiah 42:2–3).

When you're feeling bruised, God will not bruise you further. When you're crushed, He won't crush you more. If the fire in your heart has almost gone out, He won't quench it. In fact, God will fan it until it burns again. That's hope—and that's what God will do for you. "Let us then approach the throne of grace with confidence, so that we may receive mercy and find grace to help us in our time of need" (Hebrews 4:16).

The enemy, of course, will try to paint a different picture of God in your mind—a picture of a cruel taskmaster who carries a big stick. "If you fail Him one more time," the devil will whisper to you when you're down, "God will give up on you!"

That's not the heart of Jesus. He was a human, just like you, and He knows what you're going through.

> For this reason he had to be made like his brothers in
> every way, in order that he might become a merciful and

faithful high priest in service to God, and that he might make atonement for the sins of the people. Because he himself suffered when he was tempted, he is able to help those who are being tempted.

Hebrews 2:17–18

We, too, need a vision of the future to get us through difficult times. But when you're drowning spiritually, it's all you can do to keep your head above water, never mind swimming to some distant shore. You need someone to throw you a life preserver, and then tow you to dry land. That's the job of the Holy Spirit: "May the God of hope fill you with all joy and peace as you trust in him, so that you may overflow with hope by the power of the Holy Spirit" (Romans 15:13).

Jesus said that another name for the Holy Spirit is the "Comforter," and one of His ministries is to give you hope. Today Dorothy Brookshire knows what it means to "overflow with hope." For a long, long time, however, hope was absent from her life. For fourteen years—ten of them as a Christian— she suffered from severe depression. Then one day she heard a sermon on staying strong in the Lord. The minister suggested that when you are too "down" to pray, try playing or singing along with praise and worship songs. As the music ministers to your heart, he explained, you'll be brought back to the place where you feel like worshiping.

Dorothy decided to try it. Though she was in a difficult financial situation, she felt that money spent on Christian praise and worship music would be well-invested. Even though she didn't feel like praying, she created an atmosphere of praise in her home. In turn, the Lord used the vehicle of music to bring her into His presence. There the Holy Spirit could minister to her deep needs.

Today Dorothy is completely free from depression. The inner healing that the Lord gave her has made her a new person. The key to her inner healing was spending time in the presence of God.

Paula Julian had a similar experience. This Connersville, Indiana, resident today keeps praise and worship tapes in her car. "I feel I am being spiritually fed with God's Word as I drive," she says. Singing and praising God while driving have a very special meaning for Paula because for ten long years she was afraid to drive. "But through Scripture-based music," she explains, "all the 'fear tapes' in my mind have been gradually replaced with God's Word in song! God's Word is powerful and victorious—I'm living proof."

If you are hurting, then you already know what it means to offer a "sacrifice of praise" because when we're miserable we feel least like praising God. But as we begin to worship Him, however halfheartedly, He draws us into His presence, and there He heals our hurts. Sometimes we may not be able to praise God ourselves, but if we can be around others who can—either in church or on recordings—God can still begin His healing work.

Berta Jo Mercer discovered this when her 25-year-old daughter, Kim, was killed in a car accident. Even though Berta Jo's heart was broken, she knew she had to stay close to God. The day before Kim's accident, the Mercers had received a praise and worship tape, "Mighty Warrior," in the mail. During the worst of her grief following Kim's death, Berta Jo persisted in playing the tape, allowing God to draw her into His presence and touch her with His healing balm. One song in particular, "Joy of My Desire," became very special to her:

> Joy of my desire
> All-consuming fire
> Lord of glory

Rose of Sharon
Rare and sweet
You are now my peace
Comforter and Friend
Wonderful, so beautiful
You are to me
  I worship You
  In spirit and in truth
  I worship You
  In spirit and in truth
There will never be a friend
As dear to me as you

The Lord took Berta Jo by the hand and helped her walk through what the psalmist called the "Valley of Baca":

> Blessed are those whose strength is in you, who have set their hearts on pilgrimage. As they pass through the Valley of Baca, they make it a place of springs; the autumn rains also cover it with pools.
>
> Psalm 84:5–6

The Valley of Baca was also known as the "Valley of Weeping." Throughout the valley, balsam trees grew, which in Old Testament times were highly prized because they produced a fragrant, sticky resin called balm. Balm was valued for medicinal purposes, particularly in the treatment of wounds. When the prophet Jeremiah was heartbroken over the state of God's people, he cried out, "Is there no balm in Gilead? Is there no physician there?" (Jeremiah 8:22). You, too, may pass through the valley of weeping, but God can turn it into a place of springs and refreshment.

Rosella Anderson walked through the valley of weeping, and found that God had prepared the way for her by planting trees with His healing balm along the way. One August morning Rosella returned home from driving her husband to his office in Milwaukee, and found their house in flames. Inside, she knew, were her daughter and her two grandsons. Her daughter and two-year-old James escaped, but tragically three-year-old Joshua was killed.

The only things that remained uncharred after the fire were a few items in Rosella's office—including a praise and worship tape, "Give Thanks." Each morning Rosella and her husband would play the tape in the motel room that the Red Cross had provided for them. The reassuring Scripture songs on the tape gave them strength to do what they had to do—bury Joshua, find a new place to live, and go on with the Lord. Rosella found that, in the midst of their darkest hour, praising God gave them the peace that passes all understanding.

God's Word is clear that He heeds the cry of the broken-hearted. For example:

> The Lord is a refuge for the oppressed, a stronghold in
>   times of trouble.
> Those who know your name will trust in you, for you,
>   Lord, have never forsaken those who seek you . . . .
> He does not ignore the cry of the afflicted.
>   Psalm 9:9–10, 12

We must make that cry, however. We must bring into His presence our brokenness and hurt. If we try to ignore the inner pain, if we shove it down and pretend it isn't there, it can fester inside until it erupts in physical symptoms. A backache may be the result of tension in a close relationship. A chronic headache may have its roots in hidden unforgiveness. Proverbs 17:22 says, "A cheerful heart is good medicine, but a crushed spirit dries up the bones."

Often the Lord will use these physical stresses to get your

attention. You might not even know that there is something "stewing" inside you, but once you begin to pray about the physical need, the Lord will be able to deal with the underlying problem.

In your worship time, ask the Lord to begin to show you areas in your life that need healing. You may not be aware of them, but the Lord, who wove you together in your mother's womb, knows (Psalm 139:15). As you spend time in His presence, ask Him to touch you with His healing balm. "Search me, O God, and know my heart; test me and know my anxious thoughts. See if there is any offensive way in me, and lead me in the way everlasting" (Psalm 139:23–24).

7

Power Over Satan

"To proclaim freedom for the captives."

Isaiah 61:1

"WE'RE TAKING over your sound system and this Square, and *nothing* will stop us!"

The angry young man stabbed a finger barely an inch from Jerry Brandt's face, while a dozen of his friends cheered him on. From a few blocks away came the sounds of the militant crowd they represented—1,000 angry street people, gays and lesbians who were marching down San Francisco's Market Street toward Union Square in a political demonstration.

It was 7:00 on a Friday evening in mid-March a few years ago. Jerry Brandt, head of Action Evangelism, a ministry that mobilizes churches to win cities for the Lord, had scheduled an outdoor praise and prayer service in Union Square for 8:00 that evening to kick off a drive for the homeless. Jerry had filled out all the papers necessary to reserve the Square, but the angry crowd coming down Market Street was not about to stand on formalities. It was still an hour away from the scheduled starting time of the service; only the musicians and sound crew were there—fewer than fifteen people facing a violent mob determined to take control of the Square.

"Are you in charge here?" the young man demanded of

Jerry, glaring about the platform where he was putting up microphones.

Jerry took a deep breath. "I'm second-in-command," he told him. "Jesus Christ is in charge!"

Ignoring this, the young man gestured toward Market Street. "We've got a thousand people on their way here. As soon as they get here, we're taking over the Square."

Jerry knew he had to say something, and he had to say it fast. Suddenly he felt an anointing from God. "Let me tell you something," he told the young man in front of him. "You're too late. Jesus has already taken over the Square, and we're going to lift up His name alone in this place!"

"We'll see about that!" was the young man's retort as he and the others marched off the platform and up Market Street to join the other demonstrators.

Quickly Jerry organized the handful of Christians who were with him. Some began to worship God on the platform, while others marched around Union Square praying and taking authority over the territory. Six times they walked around the Square, and on the seventh the Lord spoke to them: "Your worship and praise have filled this place with My angels. It is covered!"

They rejoined the other Christians on the platform, and as they sang louder and louder they felt the boldness of the Lord fill them. One man read from Deuteronomy 28:7: "The Lord will grant that the enemies who rise up against you will be defeated before you. They will come at you from one direction but flee from you in seven."

It wasn't long before this Scripture promise was put to the test. The angry mob, 1,000 strong, reached the foot of Market Street—the very spot where the Lord had told the Christians that the Square was covered. Jerry and the others continued singing and praising God, not looking at the crowd but focusing their eyes on Jesus.

Suddenly they realized what was happening. At the entrance to the Square, the marchers had stopped in their tracks, turned, and headed the other way, almost treading on each other's heels!

"God promised us deliverance," Jerry says, looking back on that night, "and the power of praise activated it. In our work ministering on the streets, we've found praise and worship to be the keys to spiritual warfare."

It was the same discovery that the Israelites had made thousands of years ago. As we saw earlier, when their dreaded enemies, Moab, Ammon, and Mount Seir, declared war on Judah, King Jehoshaphat's response was to worship the Lord. The Lord's reply was reassuring:

> "Do not be afraid or discouraged because of this vast army. For the battle is not yours, but God's. . . . You will not have to fight this battle. Take up your positions; stand firm and see the deliverance the Lord will give you."
>
> 2 Chronicles 20:15, 17

Without lifting a finger, Judah watched her enemies turn on each other until there was nothing on the battlefield but "dead bodies lying on the ground." The only weapon that Judah used was worship, overt evidence of their trust in God.

When Joshua faced the walled city of Jericho, the Lord commanded the people to march in silence around the city every day for six days, the priests bearing the Ark before them. On the seventh day, they marched around the city seven times. Then as the priests blew the trumpets, everyone broke into wild cheering and shouting, exalting the name of the Lord. And the walls of the city fell—not just crumbled, but "fell flat," so that Israel could easily run in and reclaim all that was the Lord's. Again, the weapon they used was worship, praising God as they had been commanded.

Many centuries later, Paul and Silas used the same weapon to open prison doors. They had been arrested for casting a spirit of divination out of a slave girl, causing her masters to lose their source of income. Paul and Silas ended up in the inner prison with their feet in stocks. Bound physically, they were not bound spiritually. What did they do? They praised and worshiped God. And God responded!

> About midnight Paul and Silas were praying and singing hymns to God, and the other prisoners were listening to them. Suddenly there was such a violent earthquake that the foundations of the prison were shaken. At once all the prison doors flew open, and everybody's chains came loose.
>
> Acts 16:25–26

When you're in a narrow place and feel things closing in on you, remember what Paul and Silas did. They didn't complain or murmur against God, wondering why He'd done this to them. They began to praise and worship Him, and God set them free.

When you meet spiritual opposition, remember as King Jehoshaphat did that the battle is the Lord's. If you'll stay obedient to His Word, sing praises, and give thanks to His name, God Himself will fight your battles.

Worship can conquer not only physical enemies, but also enemies in the spiritual world. When King Saul was troubled by an evil spirit, he called on the shepherd boy David to play the harp—and the music drove the evil spirit away. You can bet that David wasn't playing just any song. During his years tending sheep, he had written many songs of praise to God, and doubtless it was one of these that made the evil spirit flee.

Terry Law has taught all over the world about the spiritual weapons referred to in 2 Corinthians: "The weapons we fight with are not the weapons of the world. On the contrary, they have divine power to demolish strongholds" (2 Corinthians 10:4).

Terry reminds audiences that flock to hear him that Satan and his agents conduct a ceaseless warfare aimed at undermining, controlling, and destroying lives. But God has given us weapons that we can use to counterattack Satan and his minions: the Word of God, the name of Jesus, and the blood of Jesus. Terry calls these the "mightiest, most powerful forces available to mankind." He adds that there are four "launching vehicles" that send these weapons into action against the devil: prayer, testimony, preaching, and praise and worship. These launch rockets transport the weapons so that they can smash enemy strongholds.

As you activate these weapons, you actually tap into the heavens to get supernatural assistance, oftentimes in the form of angels. God intends for the Church to participate in the outworking of His plan for the earth; the angels of God are waiting to do the will of the Lord, but they won't move until you wield your weapons.

Like David battling Goliath, you can use these principles of spiritual warfare to overcome the personal "giants" that you face each day. David was an unknown, seemingly unprepared teenager who took on the greatest military champion of his day. As Terry Law points out, the key to David's victory was something he had learned years earlier while he played his harp as he tended sheep. During this time of preparation,

God was revealing to him the principles of praise and worship, and the priority they should hold in his heart.

David recorded what he learned in the Psalms, and Terry notes that Psalm 61:8 is the key to David's great faith and courage: "Then will I ever sing praise to your name and fulfill my vows day after day." David committed himself to make praise a *daily* habit, to adopt it as a spiritual discipline. It's no wonder that when he faced a giant, he knew exactly what to do.

The first step David took was to *say* it. While others scoffed, he said, "Let not your heart fail you; I'll go and fight him," and, "You come to me with sword and spear, but I come in the name of the Lord of hosts" (1 Samuel 17:32, 45). The second step he took was to *do* it. In the natural world, power comes before the act, but in the supernatural world, it comes with the act. The third step was to *tell* it. David dragged Goliath's head back to Saul to show his nation what God had done for them.

When you face "giants" in your life, try following the steps that David used. As the song "Above All Else" declares, you'll be able to say,

> You are exalted, Lord
> Above all else
> We place You at the highest place
> Above all else
> Right now where we stand
> And ev'rywhere we go
> We place You at the highest place
> So the world will know
> > You are a mighty warrior
> > Dressed in armor of light
> > Crushing the deeds of darkness
> > Lead us on in the fight
> > Through the blood of Jesus
> > Victorious we stand
> > We place You at the highest place
> > Above all else in this land

This warfare is unavoidable once we make a commitment to Jesus. It's been going on since before human history began and is part and parcel of the Christian walk. Satan—Lucifer—was originally one of the three great archangels in heaven, entrusted with the worship of God. When he tried to turn that worship toward himself, he and the rebelling angels he commanded were thrust out of heaven. Lucifer's goal, however, remained the same. In the desert he tried to trick Jesus into worshiping him. And his mission today is still to attract worship to himself. So whenever we worship the true God, we automatically set in motion a spiritual conflict with Satan.

In late summer 1987, residents of southeast Alabama were horrified at a rash of teenage suicides in Valley and neighboring towns. Rick Hagans, a Southern Baptist minister, knew there was a satanic cult in the area. In ministering to young people, he learned that the demonic activity associated with that cult was connected with the deaths.

"Some of the kids told me about a ring of devil worshipers," he says. "A friend of theirs, one of the most popular boys in the class, had told them he was involved in a 'club' that he wanted to get out of, but the leaders wouldn't let him. He said if he was found dead, they would know that the club members had killed him." The boy was later found in a car with a hose from the exhaust pipe taped to his wrist. His death was ruled suicide by asphyxiation.

Rick decided to mobilize other Christians to get to the source of the suicides. They talked to the chiefs of police in two towns, and found that the cult members were drawing names of other students and targeting them for suicide. "If the student didn't commit suicide," Rick reports, "the group would kill him." Apparently a number of adults were also involved in the ring, including—incredibly—some ministers.

Rick and the other Christians told the police they wanted to help in any way they could. They knew it was a spiritual battle, so every day for a week they went to Valley and walked up and down the streets, praying and singing songs, carrying a twelve-foot cross, passing out tracts, talking with people. "The more we learned," Rick says, "the more evidence we saw of devil worship. The police even showed us a graveyard scattered with animal bodies used in satanic sacrifices. They told us that human bodies, too, had been dug from graves for these ghoulish rituals."

The story of Elijah in 1 Kings 17–18 became Rick's key Scripture. He recalled how Elijah had challenged the false prophets of Baal: They were to call on their gods while he called on his God; the one who answered would be the true and living God. Each side built an altar and prayed for fire from heaven to come down on it. The false prophets prayed all day but nothing happened. Then it was Elijah's turn. First he poured water over the wood on his altar until everything was drenched. Then he stood back and prayed. The Lord answered by sending flames that consumed every bit of wood. Convinced, the people fell on their faces and worshiped the true God.

Rick decided on a similar confrontation. By now it was October, so Rick got on local radio and TV stations and challenged those involved in the satanic church to meet him at midnight on Halloween in the graveyard. Rick wanted a showdown—just as Elijah had. On Halloween night Rick and 25 other Christians from different area churches met at the graveyard.

"As a street evangelist," explains Rick, "I've always fought the devil with prayer and preaching the Word, and that was what I planned to do that night. We had our twelve-foot cross and a bag of tracts. But the Lord told us otherwise. He said, 'Erect the cross and hang lanterns on either side so that it can be seen, and then just praise and worship Me.' I protested to myself because I'm not a singer, but that's what the Lord told us to do. Because there were people from different church backgrounds, we sang songs everyone would know, such as 'Just As I Am' and 'The Old Rugged Cross,' plus many Scripture choruses."

The enemy tried in every way that he could to distract the group. For example, one of the Christians found the remains of a cow that had been sacrificed. "This was miles from any pastureland," Rick points out, "so the cow could not have wandered there by accident. But the Lord told us not to pay any attention to that, just focus on Him in praise and worship." Soon a crowd gathered around the singers, jeering and taunting them. "They were dressed in Halloween costumes as ghosts and vampires, so it was pretty eerie," says Rick. "We didn't know if they were part of the satanic cult or just curious onlookers. But the Lord told us to keep on praising Him. We didn't even pray warfare-type prayers or break curses or strongholds. All we did was praise and worship the Lord."

And as they did so, God's Spirit captivated the crowd. They stayed for hours to watch and listen. "They weren't watching a bunch of professional musicians," laughs Rick. "It wasn't Dallas Holm out there. We didn't even have a guitar. It was the Spirit of God they were seeing."

At midnight, the Christians took Communion. Rick knew that devil worshipers blaspheme the Lord's Supper with rituals of eating human flesh, so he knew holy Communion would be a powerful witness.

At the close of the meeting, the Christians began to share the Gospel with the onlookers. The crowd stayed until 4:00 in the morning listening to the Word of God.

Something happened that night in southeast Alabama—and something in the heavenlies—because since that night there have been no more suicides in the area.

Declaring God's Word, Jesus' blood, and Jesus' name in praise releases great victory against the powers of darkness. Psalm 149 says, "May the praise of God be in their mouths and a double-edged sword in their hands" (verse 6).

Ephesians 6:17 tells us that the sword of the Spirit is the Word of God. When you sing Scriptures, you're launching powerful weapons that the enemy can't counter. You're doing warfare because you're declaring the name of Jesus, the resurrection and sovereignty of Jesus, and the fact that He has already defeated Satan. You're using the truths of Jesus to fight the lies of Satan. When you sing,

> Come into the Holy of Holies
> Enter by the blood of the Lamb
> Come into His presence with singing
> Worship at the throne of God
>
> Lifting holy hands
> To the King of kings
> Worship Jesus, worship Jesus

you are quoting Hebrews 10:19, which sets forth the authority of the blood of Jesus. And when you declare in song,

> We are victors
> We are conquerors
> We have triumphed through
> The blood of Jesus Christ
> > Victors in Christ
> > Victors, we reign forever
> > Victors in Christ
> > Life conquers death evermore

you are repeating the battle cry of 1 Corinthians 15:57. And when you sing,

Now unto Him who is able
To keep you from falling
And to make you stand
In His presence
Blameless and with great joy

To the only God our Savior
Through Jesus Christ our Lord
Be the glory and the majesty
Dominion and authority
Both now and ever
Amen!

you are declaring the praises of God from Jude 24–25.

Penny Baker has a ministry to people living on remote islands in the Pacific and in Indian villages of Alaska and Canada. She has found that even Christians there are often under a spiritual heaviness because of the demonic traditions of these areas.

"Praise and worship are practically nonexistent in these localities," she says, "and what is there does not have much anointing." About half-an-hour before she begins a service, Penny puts on a praise and worship tape. "Soon the people are singing and clapping to the songs, praising God and worshiping Him," she says. "Consequently, their hearts are prepared to receive the Word, and the anointing in the music sends demonic spirits fleeing. Then I teach the people the songs, leaving them a tool that they can use to combat the demonic folklore of their ancestors."

T.L. Osborne, an evangelist who has led people to the Lord all over the world, held a healing and deliverance crusade in Mombasa, Kenya, where he saw the power of praise and worship in a mighty way. Thousands of people came from villages all around Mombasa, and with them they carried the sick and dying—on stretchers, in wheelchairs, on their backs.

Half-an-hour before each service began, twenty loudspeakers all over the field played music from the tape "All Hail King Jesus." Even though most of the people didn't understand English, they were still touched by the anointing of the Holy Spirit as the tape played.

> Praise to the King
> Who reigns in righteousness
> Glory to the Master
> Reigning on the throne
> Worthy, Master
> Worthy of honor
> Holy, holy
> Precious and loving are You

"They'd never heard music like this before—never," T.L. says. "What must it feel like to be sick and diseased, with no hospital, no medicine, no doctor, nobody to help you—and then to be carried in from the country and set down on the ground and hear music like that come out over those big speakers? It's like heaven to them. No wonder! Jesus is there!"

T.L. adds that as music played during the crusade, particularly the song "We're Standing on Holy Ground," they could actually hear demons screaming. "By the power of God," he declares, "we took control of the atmosphere and prayed down the Kingdom reign over that field. No wonder the demons screamed—if I belonged to Satan I'd scream when that music came over the speaker! When the presence of God is released in that way, anything can happen."

Perhaps in your life you are facing battles that seem beyond your strength—a broken marriage, a runaway child, a hopeless financial future. You may sense that the devil has a stranglehold on you or on the person you've been praying for. One way to defeat him is to praise God in song: The battle that's too hard for you is never too hard for Him. Remember that the devil cannot stay around long where the name of Jesus is lifted up!

8

Power to Heal

"To proclaim . . . recovery of sight for the blind."
Luke 4:18

DORENE BRANSON of Boise, Idaho, had lupus, a debilitating disease that was slowly destroying her joints, kidneys, and bladder. Dorene had suffered from lupus for years, but she believed God wanted to heal her—in His timing and for His glory. When she received a copy of the tape "Give Thanks," she played it over and over again until she had every word memorized, especially the lines to the song "I Am the God that Healeth Thee":

> I am the God that healeth thee
> I am the Lord, your Healer
> I sent My word and healed your disease
> I am the Lord, your Healer
> You are the God that healeth me
> You are the Lord, my Healer
> You sent Your word and healed my disease
> You are the Lord, my Healer

One cold January evening, Dorene was at her prayer group when the others said they felt the Lord wanted them to pray for her. They did not know that Dorene had been in pain all month and was losing use of her right arm because her wrist and shoulder were deteriorating.

As they anointed her with oil and began to pray, Dorene could feel the power of God. She knew He was doing something, and believed she heard Him tell her to pray healing Scriptures for a week, standing on His Word. She had a copy of *Scripture Keys for Kingdom Living* by June Newman Davis, and every day prayed the Scriptures under the healing category.

The next week Dorene went to her doctor for an examination—and he could find no trace of the lupus! Not only that, but all her joints and muscles that had deteriorated were back to normal, as were her kidneys and bladder. Doctors were dumbfounded!

There have been many testimonies of God's healing power released as people listened to the "Give Thanks" tape. Don Moen, who wrote the song "I Am the God that Healeth Thee," based on Exodus 15:26, has seen the miraculous healing power of God descend during live performances, too. This Scripture, he points out, was the word of the Lord to Moses and the people of Israel, and it came after they had escaped Pharoah and his army, and were dancing and singing in gratitude before the Lord:

"If thou wilt diligently harken to the voice of thy God, and wilt do that which is right in his sight, and wilt give ear to his commandments, and keep all his statutes, I will put none of these diseases upon thee, which I have brought upon the Egyptians: *for I am the Lord that healeth thee.*"

KJV, emphasis added

God is a healing God! He said it Himself—not only in Exodus 15:26, but also in many other Scriptures throughout the Old and New Testaments:

He sent forth his word and healed them;
  he rescued them from the grave.

Psalm 107:20

Surely he took up our infirmities
  and carried our sorrows . . . and by his wounds we are
  healed.

Isaiah 53:4–5

Heal me, O Lord, and I will be healed
  . . . for you are the one I praise.

Jeremiah 17:14

He [Jesus] . . . healed all the sick. This was to fulfill what
was spoken through the prophet Isaiah: "He took up our
infirmities and carried our diseases."

Matthew 8:16–17

"Heal the sick."

Matthew 10:8

Now to each one the manifestation of the Spirit is given
for the common good. To one there is given . . . gifts of
healing.

1 Corinthians 12:7–9

Since "Jesus Christ is the same yesterday and today and
forever" (Hebrews 13:8), then it's still His nature to heal! God
is still in the healing business. There's nothing secret or
mysterious about it. It's not a special formula or set of prayers
that you have to say. Just as you cannot earn your salvation,
you cannot earn your healing. God is the Healer. As we draw
near to His presence, His healing power will be present to
heal. Luke 5:17 notes, "The power of the Lord was present for
him to heal the sick."

In a ten-year period, Elizabeth Ashcraft of Pierson, Florida, had fifteen TMJ surgeries to correct an improper joint function in her jaw. Her face was rebuilt with steel and doctors told her that she would never be able to sing. Recently she and her family drove forty miles to buy some praise and worship music tapes. When she began playing the tapes, she opened her mouth and the implants stopped grinding. For the first time in ten years, Elizabeth could sing—and she's been singing every day since.

When you praise God, you declare His attributes as Healer. And, as Dorene Branson discovered, when you use Scriptures to do so, you add "punch" to your praise. When you sing, "You are the God that healeth me," you are making a declaration that Jehovah Raphah, the God who heals, is still in the healing business. You are telling the devil that no matter how much he desires to destroy and kill, God's will for your health is stronger still.

Imagine the spiritual power unleashed when a roomful of people sing about the healing majesty of God! The Scriptures talk about a geometric progression of this power:

> "You will pursue your enemies, and they will fall by the sword before you. Five of you will chase a hundred, and a hundred of you will chase ten thousand."
>
> Leviticus 26:7–8

Suppose your doctor determines that your symptoms are the result of a malignant tumor affecting your central nervous system. He tells you the name of it, and writes it out on a piece of paper: neuroblastoma. Looking at that name scrawled on a piece of paper might produce in you a natural reaction: fear!

"I can't even pronounce it!" you might protest. "How can I pray about it?"

No matter how complicated or ominous the medical name for a disease may sound, the name of Jesus is above it, for God "has put everything under his feet" (1 Corinthians 15:27). "And God placed all things under his feet" (Ephesians 1:22). When you praise God, you're declaring that everything— even neuroblastoma—is under the feet of Jesus.

A woman we'll call Dierdre, who lives in Webster Groves, Missouri, knows this very personally. Dierdre's doctor detected several large lumps in her breast. Dierdre knew she had a choice—to give in to fear and listen to the lies that the enemy was telling her, or to believe the truth that Jesus was master even of this situation.

Dierdre chose the truth, and started warring against Satan by singing and playing praise and worship music. A friend in her prayer group gave her a copy of "Give Thanks," and Dierdre played the tape in her car everywhere she went for an entire week. She didn't feel as though anything was happening, but she kept at it. The day that she was to go to another doctor for more tests, she suddenly felt such an anointing that she knew she was going to come out of the situation victorious.

When she went in for this second examination, the new doctor could not find any lumps. Her own doctor wrote in his medical records, "Healed by God."

As with all praise, sacrifice may be involved. When King David begged God to remove a plague from the land, the Lord told him to build an altar on the threshing floor of a man named Araunah. Araunah offered to give the king his property without charge. But David said to him, "No, I insist on paying you for it. I will not sacrifice to the Lord my God burnt offerings that cost me nothing" (2 Samuel 24:24). He bought the property for fifty shekels of silver, built an altar on it, and offered a sacrifice to God, who stopped the plague from destroying Israel.

David did not want to offer a sacrifice that cost him nothing. There's not much of a sacrifice involved in that. When you pray for healing, many times it's a sacrifice. It takes faith to sing, "I am the God that healeth thee" when you're in pain. You may have prayed for weeks, months, even years for God to heal you. The devil may be yelling in your ear that you're a liar for praising God. Your friends and family may be telling you the same thing!

That's when God wants you to offer a sacrifice of praise and thanksgiving. Now, there's no reason to exclaim, "Thank You, God, for my cold!" because God didn't give you your cold. The devil did. He came to kill and destroy. Sickness is part of the curse. But Jesus came to give you life—abundant life. So that's what you praise Him for. You can say, "God, I feel awful. My nose is so sore from blowing it that it feels as if it's going to fall off. But in the midst of this affliction I praise You. Your Word is still true. You still are a God who heals."

Lynn Bolduc of New Port Richey, Florida, has prayed that way. Not long ago, Lynn's brother was diagnosed as having AIDS. Lynn flew across the country to be with him, bringing a copy of her "Give Thanks" tape with her. With the help of the Scripture songs on the tape, Lynn was able to share the Gospel with her brother and lead him to salvation. God even healed lesions on her brother's brain that were causing him severe headaches.

But two months after Lynn's trip, her brother died.

Lynn could be angry at God, refusing ever to praise Him again. But she chose to thank Him that her brother accepted the Lord and is now with his heavenly Father.

Earlier in the book we looked at how Moses drew near to

God in spite of the "thick darkness," while the people hung back in fear (Exodus 20). When you're confronted with a negative prognosis, it's natural to be afraid.

But if you want to be a "God-pleaser," you must rise above that fear in faith. Faith doesn't come when you can see everything in front of you. Faith comes when you look at that doctor's report and say, "I'm *still* going to believe God."

King Jehoshaphat received a bad report that "a vast army" was coming against him (2 Chronicles 20). The Bible says very frankly that Jehoshaphat was "alarmed" (verse 3). But it goes on to say that immediately he "resolved to inquire of the Lord." And God delivered him and his nation.

You can follow Jehoshaphat's example. Keep your eyes on Jesus, not on your sickness. Begin to praise God for who He is. Remind Him of His many blessings to you, and tell Him that the devil is trying to steal them away. "God," you might pray, "the devil is trying to hit me with this illness. He's trying to steal the blessings of good health that You've promised me. Lord, even though I'm in pain, I praise You and thank You for Your promises. I may not feel that I'm healed, but according to Your Word I already am. By Jesus' stripes I am healed. I know what Your promise says to me, that You've already fought my battles and healed my diseases on Calvary. So I'm going to rejoice and give You all the praise and honor with a loud voice!"

Two families in different parts of the country witnessed this Scripture principle at work—Ted and Lisa Misiewicz of Mobile, Alabama, and Dale and Elyse Congelliere of Mission Viejo, California.

Ted and Lisa's daughter Hannah was born on September 8, 1988, with a severe heart defect. Three days later, she was rushed by jet ambulance to the University of Alabama at Birmingham Hospital, where she underwent surgery. Complications followed, and the next two weeks were very critical.

Before surgery, Hannah was put on a respirator. After the operation, she was purposely drugged so that she would not move—not a finger or even an eyelid. In fact, for the first two days after surgery, she was unconscious. By the third day, she was able to move, but because she was still on a respirator, she could not make any sounds or noises. Even when she cried, she didn't make a sound; only the expression on her tiny face told of the pain she was feeling.

The Cardiac Intensive Care Unit (CICU) where Hannah recovered was an enormous room, almost an entire floor of the hospital. There were six or eight other patients near Hannah's bed, mostly adults, recovering from heart transplants and bypass surgery. On any one shift, almost 45 doctors and nurses were on duty.

Ted and Lisa were allowed to see Hannah only four times each day, for ten minutes at a time. "During one visit," Ted remembers, "we saw one of the nurses playing a nursery lullaby tape for Hannah. We immediately thought of Hosanna! Music, and the next day called Integrity's offices in Mobile. They sent us a copy of 'Give Thanks' and the instrumental tape 'Peace' by overnight mail. As soon as we started playing the tapes at Hannah's bedside, we began to notice a change in the atmosphere around her."

"You could see the change in her eyes," Lisa confirms. "The nurses, too, told us that she was different when they played the praise and worship music. If she would start to cry, they would run to put on one of the tapes."

Because the CICU was so crowded, many people heard the tapes, opening the door for Ted and Lisa to share their faith in God.

Nine days after surgery, Hannah was still in critical condition, and was going downhill. At least three different times, her heart rate dropped so low that the doctors thought she was dying. "It was so difficult for us," Lisa says. "I was just numb. Finally one morning the Lord told me, 'Don't go see her tonight. Let Ted see her.' It was the hardest thing I ever had to do."

When Ted went back to see Hannah that afternoon, Lisa did not go. "I was crying and praying," she says, "when I saw a vision of Jesus standing over Hannah's crib. I couldn't see His face, but I saw His long white robe." Lisa knew the Lord was saying He was going to visit Hannah that night. She also knew that whichever way it went—whether Hannah lived or died—it was going to be the turning point. In her heart, however, she believed the Lord was saying He was going to take Hannah that night, that her healing would be in heaven. Needless to say, Lisa was devastated.

When Ted returned from the hospital, he said that Hannah looked at him as if to say, "I'm so tired." He, too, agreed that the Lord seemed to be telling them He was ready to take her home. Their late afternoon visit only confirmed what they feared; Hannah looked worse than ever—pale, exhausted, and unresponsive.

That evening Ted and Lisa received a phone call from their pastor and his wife, Michael and Jean Louise Adams, in Mobile, who were praying with some friends from church. Ted and Lisa told them what they felt the Lord was saying.

After they hung up, Michael and Jean Louise told the group in Mobile and they immediately began to pray: "Lord, help Ted and Lisa accept this. If You must take Hannah, take her quickly and without pain."

After awhile one of the men in the group said he believed they were praying the wrong kinds of prayers. They were accepting defeat, when they should stand up to the enemy and claim victory for Hannah. Suddenly the spiritual atmosphere went from mourning to rejoicing. For two hours the group in Mobile praised and worshiped God, singing and praying with a boldness many of them had never known before.

Ted and Lisa were not aware of these new prayers being said on Hannah's behalf. Sometime during the middle of that sleepless night, Ted got out of bed and looked outside. "I saw a very bright star, and then a vision of Hannah in the hospital room with all the wires and tubes still attached to her little body. But in the vision she was standing up in her crib, praising and worshiping the Lord." Ted heard the Lord tell him that he and Lisa needed to be doing the same thing— standing up and praising the Lord.

The next morning at the hospital Hannah looked "so peaceful, almost as if she really weren't there, as if she were getting ready to go with the Lord," Lisa remembers. "We didn't think she had a chance. Everyone saw us weeping, and Patty and Susan, two of the nurses, were crying too. They drew the curtains around us so that we'd have some privacy, and they let us stay forty minutes instead of the usual ten. We told Hannah that if the Lord wanted her to come home with Him, then she'd have to go."

As they prayed, they were listening to the "Give Thanks" tape, when suddenly the words to "I Am the God that Healeth Thee" struck them. "I realized what we were saying wasn't right," Ted says. "The Lord showed us that she was still with us and still holding on, and that as long as she was holding on, we had to, too."

"That was the turning point," Lisa adds. "God gave us grace to persevere and keep praying for her."

And ever so slowly, Hannah started to get better. Her progress was piecemeal, but eventually she was allowed to return to Mobile, where she was placed in another ICU at the

University of South Alabama Hospital. After six weeks, she was taken off the respirator, and then finally allowed to go home. Today, although Hannah is small for her size and still faces more surgery, she is growing steadily and does everything that other babies her age do. Adds Lisa, "I talked recently with a mother whose baby has been through what Hannah went through and her child is still experiencing many problems. It's only by the grace of God that Hannah is doing so well." Ted and Lisa both believe that praise and worship music was the biggest part of their daughter's healing. "Even when the medicine had her so drugged," says Lisa, "the music was still feeding the Word of God into her spirit."

"When I think about the vision I had," says Ted, "of Hannah standing in her crib and praising the Lord with the wires and tubes still attached to her, I feel she's been giving praise to Him through all of this."

Dale and Elyse Congelliere have a similar exciting testimony about their son. When Phillip was born on May 20, 1987, doctors detected a heart murmur. Since that's a relatively common non-life-threatening condition, Dale and Elyse were not overly concerned. But eight days after his birth, Phillip suddenly turned very pale and went into shock. The diagnosis this time was severe heart failure.

As the doctors administered oxygen, one of the nurses, a Christian, anointed him with olive oil and prayed for him. Two days later when his condition stabilized, Phillip had heart bypass surgery. Complications set in, including pneumonia, and he had to remain in the hospital.

During those first few weeks of Phillip's fragile life, Elyse's mother gave them a Scripture that she felt was a promise for Phillip:

> Blessed is he who has regard for the weak; the Lord delivers him in times of trouble. The Lord will protect

him and preserve his life; he will bless him in the land
and not surrender him to the desire of his foes. The Lord
will sustain him on his sickbed and restore him from his
bed of illness.

Psalm 41:1–3

The Congellieres held onto this Scripture promise, reading
it over and over again. The doctors said the worst was behind
him, and that he wouldn't have to have more surgery for
another two or three years.

Yet he did not get any better. In fact, he seemed just as sick
as ever before. "On one occasion I left the room to get his
bottle ready," says Elyse, "and came back and he was in
failure, gasping for air. As I called the paramedics, I held him,
crying and praying, 'Lord, don't let this be his last breath.'
Dale and I were both emotionally and physically exhausted."

Phillip was two months old when the Congellieres took him
to a team of cardiologists in San Diego, 75 miles from their
home. By the time Phillip got to their offices, he was in such
bad shape that they couldn't stabilize him. It was as if he was
drowning in his own fluid, his lungs were so full. Doctors
usually wait until babies with heart problems are two or three
years old before performing surgery because the procedure is
so delicate, but they had no choice with Phillip. Even though
immediate surgery at his young age would drastically lessen
his chance for survival, the doctors decided to go ahead with
surgery—without even stabilizing him.

The news after the surgery was not good. The doctors told
Dale and Elyse just how complex—and critical—their son's
condition was. In fact, they'd seen only one other baby with
similar defects, and he continued to have many problems.
They added that they couldn't promise what quality of life
Phillip would lead—if he lived at all.

The Congellieres were devastated by this new diagnosis, especially considering they had been told only a few months earlier that the worst was over. Each time they looked at their son, they were shocked. His fragile body had eleven pumps feeding different medications into it, a pacemaker, and many other tubes and wires monitoring every function. In addition, the doctors had purposely paralyzed his body so that he would not accidentally pull them out. His bed was so surrounded by equipment that they could hardly approach his crib. Two full-time nurses monitored him—one just to write down what the other was doing. He also had a full-time doctor at his bedside, and a cardiologist examining him regularly.

The first time that Phillip was in the hospital, while he was still a newborn, Elyse's mother had suggested that they play worship music for him. She and Dale had tried this a few times, but Elyse admits they were a little timid about continuing, not knowing how the many people who always seemed to be in the ICU would react. Slowly they had dropped the practice, relying on the Christian nurses whom God always seemed to provide to offer spiritual support. But while Phillip was in the hospital in San Diego, Dale and Elyse heard a message by Bible teacher Jack Hayford about the power of praise. "Praise," he stressed very simply, "is healing."

Dale and Elyse decided once again to play praise and worship music for Phillip. They brought a tape recorder and some tapes to his crib, particularly "Arise and Sing," which contained a song they felt was for Phillip:

> See His glory
> See His glory
> See His glory come down
> Praise His name
> Heaven reigns
> See His glory come down
> See His glory come down

And since they weren't permitted to remain with Phillip 24 hours a day, they made their own tapes telling Phillip how much they loved him, and that God was going to heal him as Psalm 41 promised, and that he needed to be strong and brave. They read him Scriptures, and even recorded the voice of his sister, Jessica, on the tape.

When the time came for the doctors to remove Phillip's respirator, his lungs were not strong enough for him to breathe on his own. The doctors adjusted the doses of the many medications he was taking, but nothing seemed to work.

"Our faith followed the movements of the monitors attached to Phillip's body," admits Elyse. "When the monitors started dropping, so did our spirits. And if the numbers went 'haywire,' we did, too."

Finally Elyse came to the end of her rope, both physically and emotionally. One morning as she was getting ready to make the long drive down to San Diego to be with Phillip, her mother offered to go with her. "I knew what kind of state I was in," Elyse remembers, "and I didn't want to drag my mother down with me. She'd been such a source of spiritual encouragement to Dale and me during the entire ordeal, and we needed her to stay strong." But her mother insisted on going with her.

All the way to the hospital, Elyse and her mother played praise and worship music, particularly "Arise and Sing."

"We played that tape over and over again all 75 miles to San Diego," Elyse says, "and by the time we got there, instead of Mom feeling depressed the way I was, she had brought me up. We walked into that hospital room strong and courageous with our spiritual armor on!"

It wasn't long before Elyse's resolve was tested. Phillip's doctor called her aside and told her that Phillip was not responding. "He said we needed to face the possibility of losing Phillip," she says.

Elyse's spirits started to sink again, but all of a sudden something in her rose up, and she told the doctor, "No, he's not going to die! I don't want you to say that again. The Lord's going to heal him!"

The nurses were very quiet. They knew Phillip was slipping, and they weren't sure how Elyse would handle it. Elyse, on the other hand, knew that all of them would not understand spiritual terms, so she turned to them and said simply, "And I want only positive thoughts around his bed!"

Elyse taped Scripture verses over Phillip's crib, and a doctor warned her bluntly, "There aren't going to be any miracles."

"I knew I couldn't look in two different directions anymore," she explains. "I had to look to the Lord and forget what was going on around me. My mother and I played the tape the entire day and continued to pray and intercede for Phillip."

At the end of the day the doctor who had been so pessimistic that morning came into the Intensive Care Unit where Phillip was hanging onto life. After examining him, he told Elyse that Phillip seemed to be responding to treatment.

"The doctor said, 'I think we've hit on something,'" Elyse laughs, "but we knew better!" It was the turnaround that Dale, Elyse, and countless prayer warriors had been praying for.

The following day was victorious indeed as Dale and Elyse went to the hospital together. As they continued to pray, sing, and play music for Phillip, Dale had a clear vision from the Lord. "I saw Elyse and me raising Phillip to the Lord before our church congregation," he explains. "Every hand was raised in praise to God for His victory!"

A month later Phillip was out of the hospital and back home. He had a few relapses, and one more surgical procedure to open his aorta, but Dale's vision did take place at the Congellieres' church at a service dedicating Phillip to the Lord. Today he is two years old and thriving. In May 1988 his pediatrician wrote:

> It has been many months since he has had any signs of congestive heart failure. It is felt that this problem should no longer be significant. . . . His cardiovascular status is now excellent overall and it is expected that he may never need additional intervention. . . . It is very gratifying to see a child who was so sick now thriving from all standpoints.

Recently Elyse went to a meeting of mothers of babies with heart problems. She said it was remarkable that of all the mothers there, she was the only one who spoke of God and the power of prayer and praise. And, significantly, Phillip was the only baby who was thriving—not just surviving, as some of them were. "Many heart babies are sickly and thin because all their energies go toward just getting enough air. Phillip is healthy, loves to eat, and is even fat! Some of the other babies were twice his age and only half his size. And they were still facing major surgeries in the years ahead. It is so obvious to me that God had made the difference."

Phillip is also doing well spiritually. Whenever he hears praise and worship music, he beams and claps. Dale and Elyse know that the praises, prayers, and Scriptures that they fed into his spirit are now bearing fruit.

9

Power to Proclaim

"To proclaim the year of the Lord's favor and the day of vengeance of our God."

Isaiah 61:2

THE BATTLE of Britain was underway. Night after night, air raid sirens kept Londoners dashing for shelter as German planes circled overhead dropping bombs in an attempt to claim England as part of its ever-growing empire. When Prime Minister Winston Churchill called one of many days of national prayer—this one on September 8, 1940— minister and intercessor Rees Howells decided to hold a midday prayer service. Just as he was ready to speak, Nazi planes began to pass overhead. The air raid siren sounded, and there was the frightening sound of antiaircraft fire, but he continued his message. Suddenly a wave of praise swept over the people, and their prayers for protection changed into shouts of praise that God was going to deliver them.

In his *War Memoirs*, Winston Churchill tells how he visited the Operations Room of the Royal Air Force on September 15, 1940, which he called "the culminating date" in Germany's attempt to invade England by air.

As he watched the last of his own forces fly to meet the never-ending waves of enemy squadrons, he asked the air marshal, "What other reserves have we?"

After a moment of silence, the reply came: "There are none."

Five long minutes passed as Churchill and the others watched England's dwindling forces battle the German onslaught. Suddenly there was an unexplained movement. The German bombers and fighters showed a continuous eastward movement as they turned toward home. No new attack appeared. In another ten minutes the action was over.

There was no reason why the German air forces should have turned for home at the moment that victory was so near—no reason except that Winston Churchill had called the entire country to prayer.

At first glance, Isaiah 61:2 seems like a confusing Scripture. Why did the prophet talk about both favor and vengeance in the same verse? Isn't that a contradiction?

Charles Simpson, Bible teacher and editor-in-chief of *Christian Conquest* magazine, says that it's not a contradiction when you realize that Isaiah was speaking of the *same* day. "While God's intention toward His people is favor," he says, "there is opposition that must be broken. In the same day that He shows grace toward those who have waited for His promise, He will show His anger toward those who have opposed His promise.

"In the same day that God was preparing Melchizedek to offer the covenant meal to faithful Abraham, He was also preparing a day of vengeance for Sodom. In the same day that God was preparing faithful David for victory and honor, He was preparing blasphemous Goliath for vengeance."

Charles also points out that sometimes our battles are fought in the heavens. "God must bring vengeance on some spiritual foes. We can pray, but we cannot physically deal with the unseen resistance." Daniel's prayers encountered heavenly resistance for 21 days, until God sent the archangel Michael to defeat Daniel's spiritual enemy. God's vengeance toward Daniel's enemy released God's favor toward Daniel. "When favor comes to a people and the opposition is broken," Charles continues, "there is no stopping the flow of grace and power."

Let's look at the connection between God's favor/judgment and our praise and worship. We've already referred to Psalm 22:3 a number of times; this Scripture tells us that God is enthroned on the praises of Israel. God is on the throne all the time. He never gets bigger or smaller. But as we praise Him, our awareness of Him grows larger. That's what happens when we sing, "O magnify the Lord with me." The word *magnify* simply means to enlarge the Lord in our vision. Psalm 68 explains this process—and how it relates to God's favor and judgment:

> May God arise, may his enemies be scattered;
>   may his foes flee before him.
> As smoke is blown away by the wind,
>   may you blow them away;
> as wax melts before the fire,
>   may the wicked perish before God.
> But may the righteous be glad
>   and rejoice before God;
>   may they be happy and joyful.
> Sing to God, sing praise to his name,
>   extol him who rides on the clouds—
> his name is the Lord
>   —and rejoice before him.
>
> verses 1–4

As you praise the Lord, He arises on your praises. And as He does, two things happen: He executes judgment on the wicked and He vindicates the righteous.

Stormie Omartian, creator of Christian exercise videos and

author of two books, tells about a time when she encountered spiritual opposition over the health of her daughter, Amanda. When Amanda was only four years old, a doctor diagnosed a severe eye problem, saying she would need eye surgery and would have to wear thick glasses for the rest of her life. Even with the surgery, he warned, there was a good chance that Amanda's condition would only grow worse.

"I suppressed my tears all the way home in the car so that Amanda wouldn't see and ask questions," Stormie recalls. "Once in my prayer closet, I sobbed before the Lord."

Stormie remembered the countless times she and her husband had prayed for Amanda—starting before she was born. "Over the past several years, we had hosted parents' prayer groups in our house, joining with other fathers and mothers to intercede for our children—spiritually, mentally, physically, and emotionally. I remember specifically praying for protection against debilitating diseases. And what we were facing was definitely a debilitating disease."

It seemed to Stormie that their family was the focus of a deliberate attack by the enemy. Stormie kept praying for Amanda, thanking the Lord that He is a God who answers prayers. But over the next few days whenever fear or doubt stabbed her heart, Stormie began doing something else: "I deliberately battled fear and sadness with songs of praise and worship to the almighty God whom I knew to be more powerful than anything I was facing."

She also asked everyone she met if they knew of a good children's eye specialist. Most people suggested the one she had been to, but finally someone gave her the name of another doctor at a children's hospital in Los Angeles.

"I immediately praised God for the information and for this doctor," Stormie says. "When I called the hospital and got an appointment with him, I praised God for that, too. In fact, I praised God for everything that happened until the time we entered the doctor's reception area. I even praised God for the long wait to get into his office and for what he would do for us once we saw him."

After testing Amanda, the doctor diagnosed her problem as exactly what the first doctor had described. He told Stormie, however, that he had been doing a lot of work with contact lenses for children with this problem, and had had good results. He believed Amanda would not need surgery, and that he could not only prevent her eyes from deteriorating, but actually improve them.

"I nearly got down on my knees and praised God in the examination room," Stormie laughs, "but I held together and waited until the doctor was gone before I shouted, 'Praise You, Jesus!' I knew this was the answer to my prayers."

Four years later, Amanda is doing fine. She is still wearing contact lenses, and has responded so well to treatment that the doctor has used her as an example in his lectures. She has never had a single eye infection, her eyes have improved, and she will probably never need surgery. For Stormie, she will always remember the dark night of despair, and how praising God in the midst of it sent the devil flying and brought a "year of favor" into Amanda's life

A newlywed couple from Baker, Louisiana, Ken and Carolyn Ward, also saw God announce a "year of favor" in the life of someone close to them. Ken and Carolyn had brought a box of Christian music cassettes on their honeymoon, including one titled "Mighty Warrior." On the second day of traveling, however, they accidentally left the box behind, and had only "Mighty Warrior" to listen to for the next six days.

Over and over again, they listened to that one tape, learning how to become "mighty warriors" for the Lord:

Mighty Warrior
Dressed for battle
Holy Lord of all is He
Commander-in-chief
Bring us to attention
Lead us into battle
To crush the enemy

Satan has no authority
Here in this place
He has no authority here
For this habitation
Was fashioned for the Lord's presence
No authority here

What Ken and Carolyn didn't know was that God was preparing them for a "mighty battle" in just a few days. They'd planned to spend a few days vacationing with Ken's parents, but when they arrived they were shocked to find that Ken's stepmother was suffering a nervous breakdown.

"We were so charged up spiritually from listening to that tape," Carolyn explains, "that we boldly ministered to her. She received the Holy Spirit, and although she later was admitted to a hospital for treatment, she made what the doctors are calling a remarkable recovery in just ten days. We know it was the power of praise and prayer that brought the victory."

Six days of praising and worshiping God enabled this young couple to pronounce a blessing into the life of a woman who needed it very much. Are there people in your life who need God's blessing? Praising and worshiping God will empower you to proclaim a "year of favor" on their behalf. Psalm 149 explains how this happens:

Praise the Lord.
Sing to the Lord a new song,
    his praise in the assembly of the saints.

Let Israel rejoice in their Maker;
   let the people of Zion be glad in their King.
Let them praise his name with dancing
   and make music to him with tambourine and harp.

verses 1–3

Now comes an abrupt change of tone as the psalmist switches from a joyful scene of worshipers dancing and singing before the Lord to some pretty strong statements about tearing down the rulership of wicked kings and nations:

May the praise of God be in their mouths
   and a double-edged sword in their hands,
to inflict vengeance on the nations
   and punishment on the peoples,
to bind their kings with fetters,
   their nobles with shackles of iron,
to carry out the sentence written against them.
   This is the glory of all his saints.
Praise the Lord.

verses 6–9

As you rejoice in your Maker and praise Him with your mouth, you wield a powerful sword against His enemies. Ephesians 6:17 says that the sword of the Spirit is the Word of God. As you put the Word of God in your mouth, God will execute vengeance on the forces of wickedness—vengeance that He Himself has already decreed will happen.

Look at Judges 6 for a good example of how one man's worship of God blessed his nation and judged his enemies. Israel had gone against the Lord's commandments and was worshiping false gods like Baal and Asherah, so the Lord had given them over to their dreaded enemies, the Midianites, for seven years. Finally the Lord appeared to Gideon, a member of the Manasseh tribe, and told him, "Go in the strength you have and save Israel out of Midian's hand."

Gideon's response was what our response might have been: "Who, me?"

But the Lord replied, "I will be with you, and you will strike down the Midianites as if they were but one man" (verse 16).

Pay special attention to what Gideon did next. He didn't grab his bow and arrow. He didn't organize a posse. He found a goat and some unleavened bread and worshiped the Lord.

Only then did God begin directing his warfare: "Tear down your father's altar to Baal and cut down the Asherah pole beside it" (verse 25). Gideon obeyed, and step by step the Lord led him in victory over Israel's oppressors.

Your role is not to judge either people or nations. Your role is not to execute judgment over anyone. Your role is to praise God. As you do, He will release His power to set people free and bring judgment on the wicked. You will begin to see a greater distinction between those who walk in the presence of God and those who don't. In ways that will become more definable and obvious, God will begin to grant His favor to the righteous and turn His face against the wicked. Your praises are very powerful!

Here is another Scripture that illustrates these dual aspects of God's favor and judgment:

> "Surely the day is coming; it will burn like a furnace. All the arrogant and every evildoer will be stubble, and that day that is coming will set them on fire. . . . But for you who revere my name, the sun of righteousness will rise with healing in its wings."
>
> Malachi 4:1–2

Malachi compares the day of the Lord's coming to a fire that will burn up the wicked, but purify the righteous.

Right now you may be saying, "That sounds great for some far-off day of judgment, but how will praising God help me deal with the everyday resistance I face right now? What do I do about my neighbor who complains about all the cars at our weekly Bible study? Or my boss who tells me to cheat on the company's audits? Or my relatives who laugh at my beliefs?"

Jesus answered these questions very clearly when He said:

> "You have heard that it was said, 'Love your neighbor and hate your enemy.' But I tell you: Love your enemies and pray for those who persecute you, that you may be sons of your Father in heaven. He causes his sun to rise on the evil and the good, and sends rain on the righteous and the unrighteous."
>
> Matthew 5:43–45

One of the authors of this book, Michael Coleman, tells this story from his own life that answered these same questions for him.

"I was involved in a disagreement with a group of Christians that had gone on for more than two years. We had tried resolving it every way that we could, but to no avail. Finally we reached a point where God had to move or it would grow to a more serious conflict.

"I honestly believed that they were wrong and I was right, and I prayed accordingly—that God would correct them. But the Lord rebuked me right in the middle of my prayer time.

" 'What are you praying like that for?' He asked me. 'I didn't teach you to pray like that. I taught you to pray My blessing and My mercy upon them.'

"I protested that when I did, I felt so vulnerable, because I honestly believed they needed to be corrected.

"But the Lord told me that's the way He wanted me to feel. 'I want you to trust Me,' He said. Then He reminded me of a Scripture that I hadn't thought about in a while. It was all about the power of mercy:

> Speak and act as those who are going to be judged by the law that gives freedom, because judgment without mercy will be shown to anyone who has not been merciful. Mercy triumphs over judgment!
>
> James 2:12–13

"Mercy triumphs over judgment! He showed me that this is one of the most powerful spiritual forces in the universe. When we, as Christians, pray that God will have mercy toward our enemies, and when we declare that God is good and His mercy endures forever, we actually release Him to deal with the situation. As long as we harbor judgment against someone else, we hinder the process that God wants to set in motion.

"There is great power in releasing mercy toward those who oppose you. I began to do a word study in my Bible, and found this idea repeated over and over again: *The Lord is good and His mercy is everlasting.* It's in 1 Chronicles 16:34 and 41; 2 Chronicles 5:13; 2 Chronicles 7:3, 6; 2 Chronicles 20:21; Psalm 100:5; and many other places. As I saw this and repeated the same words in my personal praise time, I experienced a tremendous release of the power of God. And, as I pronounced blessing upon those who opposed me, I sensed God breaking down barriers of opposition.

"Shortly after I started to pray and worship this way, the conflict with the group of Christians began to break. We had tried many other avenues toward reconciliation in the past, but nothing had worked. It was only when I began to declare the power of the mercy of God and to truly pray for God to bless them with prosperity and His perfect will that God did something—in the situation and in me."

Psalm 50 is a powerful passage of Scripture setting forth the proper sequence:

> "Gather to me my consecrated ones,
>   who made a covenant with me by sacrifice."
> And the heavens proclaim his righteousness,
>   for God himself is judge.
>
> verses 5–6

Then follow the pronouncements God speaks to His own people:

> "Hear, O my people, and I will speak,
>   O Israel, and I will testify against you:
>   I am God, your God.
> I do not rebuke you for your sacrifices
>   or your burnt offerings, which are ever before me.
> I have no need of a bull from your stall
>   or of goats from your pens,
> for every animal of the forest is mine,
>   and the cattle on a thousand hills."
>
> verses 7–10

God is not looking for religious rituals. There is, however, a sacrifice that He *does* desire:

> "Sacrifice thank offerings to God,
>   fulfill your vows to the Most High,
> and call upon me in the day of trouble;
>   I will deliver you, and you will honor me."
>
> verses 14–15

God gathers His covenant people because He wants to correct and instruct them. He warns them not to be caught up in the external activities of "religiosity." What He really wants is a sacrifice of thanksgiving and for them to obey Him and fulfill the vows they've made.

In the next seven verses, God addresses the wicked. To them He speaks strong words of judgment, warning that He will tear to pieces those who forget Him. Psalm 50 closes with this reassuring promise:

> "He who sacrifices thank offerings honors me, and he prepares the way so that I may show him the salvation of God."
>
> verse 23

Again you can see the pattern: God deals with His people first, purifying them and asking them to offer an acceptable sacrifice of thanksgiving and a life of good conduct. Then He brings judgment on the wicked.

You may face criticism from others that wounds you and damages your reputation. How do you handle the situation? It is not your place to judge other Christians or the world. God is the Judge. But if you offer thanksgiving to Him, He will judge situations around you and vindicate you. If you praise Him and ask Him to release mercy in your adversaries' lives, you'll tap into one of the most powerful spiritual forces in the universe.

10

Power to Comfort

"To provide for those who grieve in Zion—
to bestow on them a crown of beauty
   instead of ashes,
the oil of gladness
   instead of mourning,
and a garment of praise
   instead of a spirit of despair."

Isaiah 61:3

Dear friends,

I just want to share with you something that happened with your tape "All Hail King Jesus." I hadn't even heard all the tape yet when I brought it over to the home of my friend Norm Pomerleau. He was lying in a hospital bed at home, dismissed from the hospital with no hope— cancer spread throughout his colon, liver, and elsewhere in his body. We were praying for a miracle to heal him. A strong Christian, he was ready to believe for this miracle, but at the same time trying to help his wife by letting her know his wishes for a funeral should he not recover.

Norm could no longer use his vocal chords to speak, and time was slipping fast. They had other music tapes, but besides "I Trust in Thee, O Lord," Norm had not been able to think of the songs he wanted at his funeral. But when he heard your tape "All Hail King Jesus," he used sign language to indicate that the first two songs on the tape should be sung at the funeral. These were "All Hail King Jesus" and "Lift Up Your Heads."

On November 30, very early in the morning, we were there with Norm's entire family and his pastor, Roger Kuhn. Norm was struggling as his lungs filled with fluid. His pastor began to pray and a peace started to fill the entire room. Norm wasn't struggling anymore. We put on the tape, and it played the first four words, "All hail King Jesus," and you could see Norm's body give up his spirit. His eyes looked just as if he had greeted Jesus.

Geri Mehta
New Brighton, Minnesota

You probably discovered not long after you became a Christian that belonging to Christ doesn't mean a life without problems. You still face all the trials of the human condition; it's the way you respond to them that's different. In the testimony above, the people involved faced the death of their loved one with the peace of God and the comfort of His presence. How is this possible?

The Scripture verse for this chapter, Isaiah 61:3, is a key passage for our understanding of praise and worship. Notice that this verse concerns those who dwell in Zion. *Zion* is an Old Testament term that refers to the dwelling place of God and the people of Israel. Christians interpret it also to mean the redeemed community or the body of believers—in other words, the Church today.

You'll also see that the operative or action words in this verse, *to provide* and *to bestow,* are different from those of verses 1 and 2. In those verses, the operative words are *to preach, to bind up, to proclaim.* But in verse 3 they are *provide* and *bestow.* The writer implies that there is actually an ability to *give* to those who are grieving something very special.

No doubt you have been through times of mourning in your

life, perhaps at this very moment. Mourning occurs whenever there is a loss. It may be the loss of a loved one. Or it can be the loss of something you deeply hoped for, leaving you in great disappointment. It can even be the loss of a physical thing you were deeply attached to. Sometimes it's simply the unrelenting pressures of life that sap your strength, leaving you fainthearted and heavy.

If any of this hits home, then the Bible has good news for you as a believer!

Isaiah 61:3 promises that heaviness and despair will be replaced with gladness and beauty. God has provided a very practical antidote to mourning, sadness, and depression—a progression that is outlined in this verse. First put on a "garment of praise." Even if you don't "feel" like it, start praising God and thanking Him. As you do, God will begin to anoint you with the oil of gladness. And finally, God's presence will "beautify" you.

There's a common thread running through Scripture passages that refer to joy. Acts 2:28 says of Jesus, "You will fill me with joy in your presence." This is a quotation from Psalm 16:11: "You have made known to me the path of life; you will fill me with joy in your presence, with eternal pleasures at your right hand."

Hebrews 1:9 quotes God the Father speaking about His Son, Jesus: "You have loved righteousness and hated wickedness; therefore God, your God, has set you above your companions by anointing you with the oil of joy."

What's the common thread? The presence of God! If you want to find true, enduring joy, the only place to look is in the presence of God—around the feet of Jesus, in fellowship with Him.

Keep in mind that we're talking about joy, not happiness. They are two different things. Happiness is an emotion. The world looks for happiness, but finds it to be elusive, passing, and fading. You can be happy one moment and sad the next, because happiness is only a momentary feeling. But joy—the joy of the Lord—is eternal, because it comes out of His very nature, which never changes. When you find God's joy, you find His strength. Nehemiah 8:10 says, "Do not grieve, for the joy of the Lord is your strength."

And don't forget that praise must often be offered as a sacrifice. When we're grieving, praising God is the last thing we feel like doing. Praising God in the midst of grief is an act of obedience to God's command, and a demonstration of trust that looks beyond circumstances.

Let's look more closely at Isaiah 61:3. What does this Scripture mean when it says "ashes"? Ashes are left over when something has burned up. When you see a pile of ashes, you know something is gone and cannot be recovered. If you've ever lost something that you greatly valued, you know the pain involved. It may have been your career dreams. Perhaps you pinned your hopes on what you could do with your own business, or with your professional skills, and your efforts failed. Or maybe you had unrealistic expectations of your children, wanting them to be something that God has not called them to be. When you finally recognized this, you were left deeply disillusioned. Or you may have finally attained what you'd been going after for years—and found it empty and dry.

If you feel like this, for whatever reason, God holds out a divine exchange to you: a crown of beauty in place of the ash heap you are presently regarding.

It's also possible that the ashes are deep within. Maybe you've been under such stress that you're experiencing spiritual burnout. Your spirit and mind have grown insensitive to the Lord; you've lost your joy and you don't know why. You find yourself walking around with your head and your hands hanging down. You wonder where God is and if He even hears you anymore when you cry out to Him.

God has provided a solution for you, too: to return to an awareness of His presence through praise and worship. Psalm 100 promises that we can "enter his gates with thanksgiving and his courts with praise" (verse 4).

If you are fighting burnout, maybe one woman's weekend sounds all too familiar to you. She began her Friday night by taking a carless friend grocery-shopping. On Saturday she arose early to make breakfast for a house guest whom she dropped off at an 8:00 A.M. appointment. She quickly ran some errands, picked up her guest, and made a cake for a newcomers' dinner that evening. On Sunday morning she picked up two people for church, attended an outreach luncheon, helped her pastor compose a four-page fund-raising letter . . . and ended the day feeling that God, in whose service she'd been so busy, was a million miles away. In doing the work He had given her to do, she'd neglected her own need to spend time in His presence.

How can we find this time, in lives crowded with worthwhile and necessary activities? Like many mothers, Sally Cardella of St. Clair, Michigan, found it a constant battle to get her children dressed, fed, and out the door to school each morning. She discovered that by playing praise and worship tapes during this hectic hour, not only was her own consciousness of God's presence heightened, but there was a "marked change" in her children's behavior. "To my surprise," she says, "they were actually being pleasant to one another."

One morning she was busy making breakfast and forgot to turn the tape recorder on. "The children were miserable toward one another," she says. "I promptly went to the recorder and pushed the 'play' button. Within moments their behavior changed."

The next time that Christian burnout leaves you with a bucketful of ashes, try tackling your busy schedule against a background of joyful praise and worship songs!

A modern word for "mourning" is *depression*—and Christians are not immune from its attacks. David, a man after God's own heart, suffered from depression.

> Why are you downcast, O my soul?
>   Why so disturbed within me?
> Put your hope in God,
>   for I will yet praise him,
>   my Savior and my God.
>   Psalm 42:5–6

Job despaired of life itself, imploring God to take it from him:

> "Oh, that I might have my request,
>   that God would grant what I hope for,
> that God would be willing to crush me,
>   to let loose his hand and cut me off!"
>   Job 6:8–9

Elijah, too, experienced deep depression. Even after the great miracles of Mount Carmel, he longed for death:

> Elijah . . . came to a broom tree, sat down under it and prayed that he might die. "I have had enough, Lord," he said. "Take my life."
>   1 Kings 19:4

Have you ever been so depressed that all you wanted to do was die? Depression is the opposite of joy. It starts with discouragement and disillusionment, and can end in suicide. But God can reverse this progression, as He reversed the seemingly hopeless lot of the Babylonian captives:

> When the Lord brought back the captives to Zion,
> we were like men who dreamed.
> Our mouths were filled with laughter,
> our tongues with songs of joy.
> The Lord has done great things for us,
> and we are filled with joy.
> Restore our fortunes, O Lord,
> like streams in the Negev.
> Those who sow in tears
> will reap with songs of joy
> He who goes out weeping,
> carrying seed to sow,
> will return with songs of joy,
> carrying sheaves with him.
>
> Psalm 126:1–6

Isaiah 35:10 promises that

> The ransomed of the Lord will return.
> They will enter Zion with singing;
> everlasting joy will crown their heads.
> Gladness and joy will overtake them,
> and sorrow and sighing will flee away.

How do you get rid of sighing and sorrow? You can't, in your own strength. But God will put a song in your mouth, and as you sing it, your depression will flee.

A woman from Pennsylvania whom we'll call Denise (not her real name) prayed for many years to be free from the depression that she called a "dark prison within." One day as she was reading her Bible, the words of Psalm 40 seemed to speak directly to her:

I waited patiently for the Lord;
  he turned to me and heard my cry.
He lifted me out of the slimy pit,
  out of the mud and mire;
he set my feet on a rock
  and gave me a firm place to stand.
He put a new song in my mouth,
  a hymn of praise to our God.

verses 1–3

With the first flicker of hope in years, Denise began listening to a praise and worship music tape. The "new song" of praise that Psalm 40 promised became her own song, and kept her alive as she waited for God to heal her.

Some time later, Denise was hospitalized for tests and treatment for her depression. Her doctors diagnosed her problem as a chemical imbalance that could be corrected with medication. During the month she spent in the hospital she played her praise and worship music recordings almost continually. Today she has another psalm that she claims as her own: "He sent His word and healed me" (Psalm 107:20, paraphrased).

Denise overcame her problems by putting on a garment of praise every day. If you face situations as Denise did, clothe yourself in His praise—all the time. Don't just praise Him on Sunday mornings or on those days when you feel like it. Wear praise as you wear a garment—24 hours a day. Look again at 1 Peter 2:9:

But you are a chosen people, a royal priesthood, a holy nation, a people belonging to God, that you may declare the praises of him who called you out of darkness into his wonderful light.

1 Peter 2:9

God is in the business of bringing people out of darkness into light, a process that Jeremiah 33 outlines. Jeremiah starts by describing Jerusalem as "a desolate waste, without men or animals" (verse 10).

But in the very next verse comes encouraging news. God promises to restore

> the sounds of joy and gladness, the voices of bride and bridegroom, and the voices of those who bring thank offerings to the house of the Lord, saying, "Give thanks to the Lord Almighty, for the Lord is good; his love endures forever."
>
> Jeremiah 33:11

This quotation is a wonderful sentence to commit to memory against those moments when the "spirit of despair" casts its long shadow over your life. If you ever lack for expressions of praise, declare that the Lord is good, and that His love lasts forever.

On November 22, 1987, Marlin and Joyce Davis' three sons, Marlin, Jr. (age eighteen), Eddie (sixteen), and Matt (fifteen) were all killed in a private plane crash. All three Davis boys had been Christians; they had loved life, sports, cars, and they'd loved God. Marlin had taught a youth Bible study each Friday night. Eddie used his Jeep to bring friends to the study, and devoted time every morning before school to prayer. Matt, too, loved the Lord and brought his friends to the study.

Christian music was a big part of the Davis home. The boys often commented about the atmosphere of praise in their home, asking their mom to put on praise and worship tapes if they weren't already playing when they got home from school. Joyce and Marlin know that the music played in their home helped to prepare the boys for what they're hearing now—heavenly music.

In spite of Marlin and Joyce Davis' enormous loss, the Lord has given them a garment of praise instead of what could easily have been a spirit of despair. They witness to His faithfulness at churches, retreats, and on local television stations around Scottsdale, Arizona, where they live. They stress that less television and more Christian music as children grow up will give them a nurturing spiritual atmosphere, preparing them for whatever lies ahead.

The Lord is offering joy to you, also. Like the Davis family, no matter what heavy burden you carry, the Lord has a provision for your grief—the oil of His own gladness.

11

How to Put the Power of Praise and Worship into Your Life

RIGHT NOW you might be saying, "Sure, I'd like to live this lifestyle of praise and worship that you're talking about, but I don't know how. I know the Lord wants me to be a more dedicated Christian, and I would love to have the kind of powerful impact upon the world that Isaiah and Paul had, but I'm just an ordinary person. I'm not even sure how to praise God—not the way you're talking about."

Most of us feel this way at the outset. But remember two things. One, God created you to worship Him; if you ask Him to help you do it, He will. And two, you haven't any choice in the matter; He commands you to worship Him. Philippians 4:4 says, "Rejoice in the Lord always. I will say it again: Rejoice!" 1 Thessalonians 5:16–18 underscores it: "Be joyful always; pray continually; give thanks in all circumstances, for this is God's will for you in Christ Jesus." It's not an option, to praise or not to praise. You were made to praise God, and you're commanded to praise Him.

To help you get started, here are three practical suggestions. First, follow the biblical pattern of thanksgiving, praise, and worship. Second, say His Word back to Him. And third, create an environment of praise and worship around you wherever you spend time.

1. Follow the biblical pattern. Psalm 100, which we looked at earlier, shows the progression from thanksgiving to praise to worship:

> Enter His gates with thanksgiving,
> And His courts with praise,
> Give thanks to Him; bless His name.
> For the Lord is good;
> His lovingkindness is everlasting,
> And His faithfulness to all generations.
>
> verses 4–5 (NAS)

The Bible is very specific about how you are to approach God. You're not supposed to come into His presence squirming and nervous! He's your loving Father, and you're to come to Him with joy. Hebrews 4:16 says, "Let us then approach the throne of grace with confidence, so that we may receive mercy and find grace to help us in our time of need."

The writer of Hebrews also tells us,

> Therefore, brothers, since we have confidence to enter the Most Holy Place by the blood of Jesus, by a new and living way opened for us through the curtain, that is, his body, and since we have a great priest over the house of God, let us draw near to God with a sincere heart in full assurance of faith.
>
> Hebrews 10:19–22

Just imagine for a moment how you would want your children to approach you. If you're a dad, do you want your children to throw a barrage of complaints and requests at you when you walk through the front door after a hard day's work? Which would you prefer to hear: "Joshua hit me with his lunchbox!" and, "Can we go to the new frozen yogurt place after dinner?" Or would you rather hear, "Hi, Daddy! We're glad to see you!" followed by hugs and kisses?

And how would you feel if every time your children came to you, they arrived with shame on their faces and fear in their hearts? Of course you'd be deeply grieved because you love them and you want to be able to communicate freely and openly.

Your heavenly Father is no different. Before you hit Him with a laundry list of problems, spend time with Him telling Him you're glad to be with Him. He doesn't want to hear about your problems immediately. He knows what they are before you tell Him! In Larry Lea's popular teaching on praying an hour a day based on the Lord's Prayer, he points out that the Lord's Prayer begins with praise: "Our Father who art in heaven, hallowed be Thy name!" The first petition, "Give us this day our daily bread," does not come until a number of verses later.

So when you approach God, follow the biblical progression of offering thanks, then praise, then worship. The place to start is with thanksgiving, which simply means to count your blessings and communicate verbally to God your gratitude for what He's already done. Even in the midst of difficulty, don't focus on the situation so much that you miss the opportunity to thank God. Thank Him for the specific blessings He has poured on your life—for your health, for your family, for your job, for your relationship with Him. Cultivate a thankful attitude, and practice having a thankful heart by saying to the Lord, "Thank You, Jesus, for _____ and _____ and _____ today." If you don't feel particularly thankful, that's fine. You are obeying the Word of God and giving thanks to His name. Just keep enumerating your blessings one by one and thanking God for them out loud. It will release something as you become aware how intimately God is involved with you.

After thanksgiving comes praise, which, like thanksgiving, is an act of your will and doesn't depend on how you feel. Here you begin to declare God's attributes and His great glory. Praise Him for His faithfulness, goodness, and mercy, for the way He has sustained and delivered you. Praise Him for His great power, for His forgiveness, for His wondrous creation and all the works of His hands.

This will lead naturally into worship. Thanksgiving and praise are acts of your will, but worship is something God does. This is where He draws back the curtain and makes a way in the Spirit for you to draw very, very close to Him. It's where He invites you into a place of adoration where you do less and He does more. Thanksgiving and praise are actions you initiate. But worship is a deep communion and fellowship with the Lord.

Remember: thanksgiving first, praise second, worship third.

2. Say God's Word back to Him. The second suggestion addresses the question, "What do I say to God? I can thank Him for specifics easily enough, but I'm at a loss when it comes to praising Him." One of the best ways to praise God is to open your Bible to the book of Psalms and echo the words that David spoke to Him. Read out loud the passages of Scripture that declare God's power and majesty.

Saying God's words back to Him blesses His heart and moves you swiftly into a posture of praise. He anointed men and women of old to speak the truth and He anoints the expression of this truth today. When you say His Word back to Him, you know you're on good ground. Find the passages of praise by such biblical giants as Solomon and Moses. Read out loud the words of Mary, the mother of Jesus, to her cousin Elizabeth. Her words are a tremendous way to praise God: "My soul praises the Lord and my spirit rejoices in God my Savior" (Luke 1:46–47).

Another way to repeat God's Word to Him is to learn songs that have biblical texts for lyrics. Most praise and worship songs are based on Scripture—and there's an added bonus to singing these texts. Melody is a powerful memory aid and when combined with Scripture can help bring to mind the Word of God. Once you've learned a song, you'll be able to remember the lyrics, even years later.

Perhaps you've already experienced this. Have you ever realized that, quite unconsciously, you were humming the melody to a song? At first, perhaps, you weren't sure what the song was, but gradually words you memorized long ago came to your mind. Many times the Holy Spirit will speak to us through the lyrics of a long-forgotten song, bringing its truths to remembrance when we need them most. Michael Coleman recalls two such times:

"In 1987, I was in the midst of a particularly pressured time and concerned about some major decisions we needed to make. While going about my daily activities at home, I realized I was singing a beautiful melody. At first I didn't know what the song was, but finally recognized it as the hymn 'Be Still My Soul.' Bit by bit the lyrics began to come back to me:

> Be still, my soul!
> The Lord is on thy side;
> Bear patiently the cross
> Of grief or pain;
> Leave to thy God
> To order and provide;
> In every change
> He faithful will remain.
> Be still, my soul!
> Thy best
> Thy heavenly Friend
> Thro' thorny ways
> Leads to a joyful end
>
> Be still, my soul!
> Thy God doth undertake
> To guide the future

As He has the past.
Thy hope, thy confidence
Let nothing shake;
All now mysterious
Shall be bright at last.
Be still, my soul!
The waves and winds
Still know
His voice who ruled them
While He dwelt below.

"God spoke words of comfort and direction to me through that great hymn," says Michael. "In fact, I carry the words to that song in my Bible today because they were so meaningful to me then—and still are. It was as good as anyone coming up and giving me an individual word of guidance

"Another time we were beginning work on one of our tapes—as yet unnamed. The morning of the 'creative meeting,' which is where we pray about the direction that God wants us to take on each tape, I found myself humming a song while getting ready for work. I was struck by the power and beauty of the melody, and realized it was from a tape I had at home by the singing group Truth. The song was called 'Lamb of God,' by Twila Paris. When I went into the creative meeting later that day, I felt it was right for the tape. The others agreed, and it became the title song of that album."

Similar experiences have happened to many Christians. An accident made Dave Berland of South Gate, California, glad that he had memorized Scripture through praise and worship songs. Early one January morning, Dave was driving to work on Interstate 10 when his car slammed into the back of a van. Dave's car shot across four lanes of traffic, ran up the side of a hill, and rolled back down a ravine. Dave received a deep laceration on his head and a severed artery.

"On the operating table in the hospital," he recalls, "I was scared. I asked God to please speak to me and comfort me, and He did—through a song." Dave had recently received a copy of the tape "You Are My God." That morning as he lay on the operating table, one song in particular "God Is My Refuge," with lyrics taken from Psalm 46, kept running through his mind:

> God is my refuge
> And God is my strength
> A very present help in trouble
> Therefore I will not fear
> Though the earth be removed
> And though the mountains
> Be carried into the midst of the sea

Dave kept singing the song to himself over and over again, and he felt the Lord's presence very strongly as surgery was about to commence. "I felt as if someone had laid a hand on my chest. It was so warm, and great peace came over me. God's hand of protection was on me."

Later Dave remembered the song "Return unto Thy Rest." These words, from Psalm 116:7–8, brought him comfort:

> Return unto thy rest
> O my soul, O my soul
> For the Lord has dealt bountifully with thee, with thee
> For Thou hast delivered my soul from death, from death
> For Thou hast delivered mine eyes from tears
> And my feet from falling

"Right there in the operating room," Dave adds, "I began to be filled with His Holy Spirit and to rejoice because God had rescued me. It was so exciting to realize that I was sitting at the feet of Jesus."

This is what can happen when you put Scripture to music and memorize it. You supply your spirit and mind with Bible verses and with melodies that the Holy Spirit can use to bring them to remembrance. When you store the Word of God in your heart, you can always offer up an acceptable sacrifice of praise.

3. Create a "total environment" of praise and worship wherever you spend time. It may be your laundry room, your kitchen, your office, your car. Wherever you spend many hours a day, make it a place of praise and worship. You can do this by speaking or singing to God yourself, or you can join along with others worshiping God as you play praise and worship recordings. One of the most frequent types of testimony letters we receive at Integrity Music is from people who tell us the atmosphere of their homes has changed since they have begun playing praise and worship music. Judith Haas from Omaha, Nebraska, wrote that even her three-year-old granddaughter, Naomi, commented on the difference. The little girl had been bothered by bad dreams and was afraid of the dark. When her grandmother played praise and worship music in the house, Naomi told her happily, "The songs chase the dark away!"

Douglas Silvis, an attorney in Thomasville, Georgia, plays praise and worship music on a tape player hooked up to his office phone system. "Our clients hear this music while they are on hold," he says. "And each of us in the office has it as close as his desk throughout the day. The type of music we listen to and have our clients listen to is very important."

Douglas usually selects instrumental tapes. "They're soothing and worshipful, yet they're upbeat and refreshing," he explains.

There is something about worshiping God with other Christians, even on tape, that can purify the atmosphere and drive the devil away. He can't stand the praises of Jesus and won't stay around long to listen. A Canadian woman who teaches English in northeastern China shares her experience. "Opportunities for fellowship and encouragement are rare," she writes. "You can't imagine what a blessing this music has been to me and to Chinese Christians. Whenever I feel lonely for the Spirit-filled freedom of my home fellowship, I put on one of the tapes. I also regularly wash clothes, mop floors, and chop vegetables 'before the Lord'!"

If you're ever in a situation where you cannot participate in a live worship service, think of recorded praise and worship as a catalyst or "jump-starter" to get you worshiping God on your own.

These practical steps will help to launch you on a lifestyle of praise and worship. Are you ready to make it a daily discipline?

12

A Praise and Worship Commitment

"For as the soil makes the sprout come up and a garden causes seeds to grow, so the Sovereign Lord will make righteousness and praise spring up before all nations."

Isaiah 61:11

TO HELP you make praise and worship part of your life, we'd like to leave you with three practical "tools."

First is a formal prayer of commitment. Many people find it helpful to make a visible outward sign of their intentions; after you've read the statement below, you may want to sign and date it so that it becomes a reminder.

A Commitment to Praise and Worship

I understand that God has commanded me in His Word to praise Him. I now join my faith with millions of worshipers around the world, and make this declaration:

God, by Your grace I will:

1. Offer up a sacrifice of praise continually, that is, the fruit of my lips, giving thanks to Your name (Hebrews 13:15).

2. Bless You, Lord, at all times; Your praise shall continually be in my mouth (Psalm 34:1).

3. Give thanks to You in everything, because I know this is Your will for me (1 Thessalonians 5:18).

4. Daily perform my vow of praise so that I might sing praise to Your name forever (Psalm 61:8).

Heavenly Father, I have determined in my heart to be a worshiper. Thank You that Your Spirit is upon me; with His help I will glorify Christ in my life. In Jesus' name, Amen.

—————————————   ————————
signature   date

The second tool is a daily devotional, which you'll find beginning on page 135. Many Christians who praise and worship God with vigor in a supportive church setting on Sunday morning find it difficult to do so when they're by themselves during the week. We've designed the devotional to help you get started. Each day's session includes three Scripture readings, a "praise prompter," a prayer, and a praise and worship song.

The third practical aid is a list of resources for further study, pages 157–161. Of course, the first place you should turn is the Word of God. After that, you may want to refer to some of the many good teaching books and tapes available. They'll help you nurture your new life of praise and worship.

And finally, if we can help you in any way, feel free to write us. We'd also like to hear your testimonies of how God touches *your* life through praise and worship!

Integrity Music, Inc.
P. O. Box 16801
Mobile, Alabama 36616

It's our prayer and our assurance that God will bless you as you come and worship!

Come and Worship: A Devotional

THIS THREE-WEEK devotional will help you to get started on a lifestyle of praise and worship. After you've gone through it once, twice, five times, you will find yourself inaugurating your own worship of God each day.

Start by setting aside a block of time each day to praise and worship Him—even if it's just ten or fifteen minutes. Write it on your calendar just as you would any appointment. Be committed to it! The enemy will try to keep you away from it because he knows how important it is for you to spend time in God's presence every day. Each day includes a:

Psalm: Many people are surprised to learn that the book of Psalms, the longest book in the Bible, is actually a songbook. It's a good place to begin your daily devotional.

Scripture reading: Each day includes a chapter from Scripture. Read the chapter out loud in its entirety.

Memory verse: This can be your praise Scripture for the day. If you take the time to memorize it, you'll find it ministering to you—and to others—all day.

Praise and worship song: If you don't know the melody, make up your own or read the words aloud.

Praise prompter: Remember to follow the pattern we talked about in chapter 11: first thanksgiving, then praise, and then worship.

Thoughts: Use this space to write down the ideas the Lord gives you. At the end of the week go back and read over what you've written.

Prayer: You will want to supplement this with your personal praises and petitions.

Day 1: Jesus' Royalty

Psalm: Psalm 2

Scripture reading: Revelation 21

Memory verse: "But as for Me, I have installed My King upon Zion, My holy mountain" (Psalm 2:6, NAS).

Praise and worship song: "Come and Worship"

> Come and worship, royal priesthood
> Come and praise Him, holy nation
> Show forth His praise, show forth His power
> This is the day, this is the hour
> For this is the day that the Lord has made
> Let us rejoice and be glad

Praise prompter: Imagine that the king of a far-off country is coming to visit you in your home or office this afternoon. What will you do to prepare for his arrival? How will you greet him? Now imagine that you are going to greet the King of kings. How will you greet *Him?*

*Thoughts:*_____

_____

_____

_____

_____

_____

Prayer: Lord, help me to prepare for Your arrival today, and to see You coming in ways that I don't expect.

Day 2: Jesus, My Creator

Psalm: Psalm 104

Scripture reading: Genesis 1

Memory verse: "O Lord, how many are Thy works! In wisdom Thou hast made them all; the earth is full of Thy possessions" (Psalm 104:24, NAS).

Praise and worship song: "For the Beauty of the Earth"

> For the beauty of the earth,
> For the glory of the skies,
> For the love which from our birth
> Over and around us lies:
> Lord of all, to Thee we raise
> This our hymn of grateful praise.

Praise prompter: Do you like to garden? or fish? or hike? Do you enjoy nature? Using Psalm 104 as a guideline, write a short psalm of your own praising God for His creation. Read or sing it aloud to the Author and Creator of your faith.

*Thoughts:*_____
_____
_____
_____
_____
_____

Prayer: Father, in all that I do today, help me to glorify Your name. I want to praise You with my whole being. I offer up to You everything that I am as a living sacrifice.

Day 3: Jesus' Victory

Psalm: Psalm 18

Scripture reading: 1 Corinthians 15

Memory verse: "Thanks be to God, who gives us the victory through our Lord Jesus Christ" (1 Corinthians 15:57, NAS).

Praise and worship song: "Celebrate Jesus"

> He is risen, He is risen
> And He lives forevermore
> He is risen, He is risen
> Come on and celebrate
> The resurrection of our Lord

Praise prompter: The Scriptures say that Jesus reigns with all things under His feet. Close your eyes and picture Him seated on the throne, reigning over that impossible situation in your life.

*Thoughts:*_____
_____
_____
_____
_____
_____

Prayer: Heavenly Father, I celebrate and rejoice in the fact that You are the only true God. Thank You that Jesus is alive and reigning as King of kings and Lord of lords!

Day 4: Jesus, My Shepherd

Psalm: Psalm 23

Scripture reading: Isaiah 53

Memory verse: "The Lord is my shepherd, I shall not want" (Psalm 23:1, NAS).

Praise and worship song: "Shepherd of My Soul"

> Shepherd of my soul, I give You full control
> Wherever You may lead I will follow
> I have made the choice to listen for Your voice
> Wherever You may lead I will go

Praise prompter: If you have different versions of the Bible, look up Psalm 23, compare the different translations, and then read them aloud. Which one speaks most clearly for *your* heart?

*Thoughts:*_____

_____

_____

_____

_____

_____

Prayer: Father, thank You that You "make me" to lie down in green pastures. I will rest in You today knowing that You are able to solve any problem I'm facing right now. And as I rest in You, I will praise and worship You, for You are worthy to be praised!

Day 5: Jesus, My Provider

Psalm: Psalm 65

Scripture reading: Genesis 22

Memory verse: "The meadows are clothed with flocks, and the valleys are covered with grain; they shout for joy, yes, they sing" (Psalm 65:13, NAS).

Praise and worship song: "Savior, Like a Shepherd Lead Us"

> Savior, like a shepherd lead us,
> Much we need Thy tender care;
> In Thy pleasant pastures feed us,
> For our use Thy folds prepare.

Praise prompter: If you have a prayer partner, a friend in a Bible study, or just a close friend from church, call up him or her and read today's Scripture aloud. Then share a way that you've seen God provide for you in the past 24 hours. Together, praise God that He is your provider!

Thoughts: _____

_____

_____

_____

_____

_____

Prayer: Lord, I confess to You today that You are my provider and You are, right now, meeting every need that I have according to Your riches in glory by Christ Jesus.

Day 6: Jesus' Hope

Psalm: Psalm 71

Scripture reading: Colossians 1

Memory verse: "For Thou art my hope; O Lord God, Thou art my confidence from my youth" (Psalm 71:5, NAS).

Praise and worship song: "My Life Is in You, Lord"

> I will praise You with all of my life
> I will praise You with all of my strength
> With all of my life
> With all of my strength
> All of my hope is in You

Praise prompter: Are there situations in your life that seem without hope? Write them below. But instead of telling God why you need Him to act (He already knows!), offer Him a "sacrifice of praise," thanking Him in spite of these circumstances. Thank Him that He is still God, still seated on the throne, and still the hope of your glory.

*Thoughts:*_____

_____

_____

_____

_____

Prayer: Father, thank You for strengthening me today, for being my glory and the lifter of my head, and for allowing me to do *all* things through Christ who strengthens me.

Day 7: Jesus, My King

Psalm: Psalm 24

Scripture reading: Matthew 21

Memory verse: "Say to the daughter of Zion, 'Behold your King is coming to you, gentle, and mounted upon a donkey, even upon a colt, the foal of a beast of burden' " (Matthew 21:5, NAS).

Praise and worship song: "Hosanna"
> Hosanna, Hosanna
> Hosanna, Hosanna
> Blessed be the King
> Blessed be the King
> Blessed be the King
> Who comes in the name of the Lord

Praise prompter: Many people failed to see Jesus as King because they were looking for someone who fulfilled their idea of royalty. For one thing, no real king would actually associate with known sinners. Think back on your life before you were saved, and write down two or three instances when the King of kings came to you in an unexpected way. Then praise God that His Son chose to be a King who was a Friend of sinners.

*Thoughts:*_____
_____

Prayer: Jesus, I welcome You into my life today, and I acknowledge that You are Lord of all. You are more than a prophet, more than a good teacher. You are King of kings and Lord of lords. Hosanna to the King!

Day 8: Jesus' Dominion

Psalm: Psalm 47

Scripture reading: Zechariah 9

Memory verse: "And His dominion will be from sea to sea, and from the River to the ends of the earth" (Zechariah 9:10, NAS).

Praise and worship song: "Revival in the Land"

There's gonna be a revival in the land
There's gonna be a revival in the land
From the north, the south, the east, and the west
There's gonna be a revival in the land

Praise prompter: In the space below, write the name of a foreign country. If you have an atlas, find the map where the country is shown. Now praise God because His dominion that encompasses "the ends of the earth" also encompasses that country. Thank Him for establishing His Kingdom there and for raising up Christians to carry on His work in each city and village.

*Thoughts:*_____
_____
_____
_____
_____

Prayer: Lord, show me today a specific way that I can serve my brothers and sisters in other parts of Your Kingdom.

Day 9: Jesus, My Commander-in-Chief

Psalm: Psalm 28

Scripture reading: 2 Samuel 22

Memory verse: "I call upon the Lord, who is worthy to be praised; and I am saved from my enemies" (2 Samuel 22:4, NAS).

Praise and worship song: "Raise Up an Army"

> O God, our glorious Maker, we marvel at Your grace
> That You would use us in Your plan
> Rejoicing at Your favor, delighting in Your ways
> We'll gladly follow Your command

Praise prompter: How do you think David must have felt when he wrote these words after God had just delivered him from his dreaded enemies? Turn once again in your Bible to 2 Samuel 22, but this time instead of reading David's words aloud, sing them to the Lord. Even if you "can't" sing, ask the Holy Spirit to help you. Use the melody of a song you already know, or make up one of your own. It's a great way to bless the heart of the Lord.

*Thoughts:*_____

_____

_____

_____

Prayer: Lord, no matter what I face today, I boast in Your name! Give me victory over my enemies!

Day 10: Jesus, My Banner

Psalm: Psalm 20

Scripture reading: Exodus 17

Memory verse: "And Moses built an altar, and named it The Lord is My Banner" (Exodus 17:15, NAS).

Praise and worship song: "Go Forth"

> Rise up, you champions of God
> Rise up, you royal nation
> Rise up and bear His light abroad
> We'll reach this generation
> We've got our marching orders
> Now is the time to carry them forth

Praise prompter: Look up the word *banner* in a dictionary. Briefly paraphrase each of the definitions, then add an example for each to illustrate how Jesus is your banner. Read or sing them aloud to praise Him.

*Thoughts:*_____
_____
_____
_____
_____
_____
_____

Prayer: Lord, help me to live my life so that I lift up Your name like a banner for all around me to see.

Day 11: Jesus' Holy Spirit

Psalm: Psalm 51

Scripture reading: Romans 12

Memory verse: "Do not be conformed to this world, but be transformed by the renewing of your mind, that you may prove what the will of God is" (Romans 12:2, NAS).

Praise and worship song: "Walking in the Spirit"

> Walking in the Spirit, abiding in His mercies
> In the presence of the Lord is great joy
> Walking in the Spirit, abiding in His mercies
> At His right hand are pleasures forevermore

Praise prompter: "Jennifer, you're so patient!" "I wish I could be a servant the way you are, Sam!" Has anyone ever complimented you for something you did—something that you knew could only be from the Lord because it was contrary to your own nature? Those are the fruits of the Spirit in your life. Write an example below, then praise Jesus that He is changing you.

Thoughts: _____
_____
_____
_____
_____

Prayer: Lord, there's such a big gap between how I know I *should* be and how I know I *am*. Help me to learn to walk in Your Spirit and to respond in every situation the way You would.

Day 12: Jesus, My Refuge

Psalm: Psalm 46

Scripture reading: Isaiah 4

Memory verse: "Cease striving and know that I am God" (Psalm 46:10, NAS).

Praise and worship song: "Jesus, Lover of My Soul"

> Jesus, Lover of my soul,
> Let me to Thy bosom fly,
> While the nearer waters roll,
> While the tempest still is high:
> Hide me, O my Savior, hide,
> Till the storm of life is past;
> Safe into the haven guide;
> O receive my soul at last!

Praise prompter: Look up the word *refuge* in a concordance, and list five Scripture verses that extol this characteristic of God (for example, "Thou art my strong refuge" in Psalm 71:7). Then praise God for being your refuge by reading these Scriptures aloud.

*Thoughts:*_____

_____

_____

_____

_____

Prayer: Lord, I take refuge today in You. Your name is a strong and mighty tower. Thank You for Your protection.

Day 13: Jesus on the Throne

Psalm: Psalm 93

Scripture reading: Hebrews 1

Memory verse: "But of the Son He says, 'Thy throne, O God, is forever and ever' " (Hebrews 1:8, NAS).

Praise and worship song: "Blessing, Glory, and Honor"

> Blessing, glory, and honor, pow'r and might and dominion
> Be unto Thee, my blessed Lord
> Coming down from Your throne on high
> You died on the cross for me
> Rising from the dead You live
> To give me the victory

Praise prompter: List four concerns that have been on your prayer list for more than six months—an unsaved family member, a financial need, or the like. Now praise God that in spite of these continuing needs, Jesus is still on the throne, and still actively involved in the affairs of men.

*Thoughts:*_____

_____

_____

_____

_____

_____

_____

Prayer: Lord, every time today that I'm tempted to worry, please remind me that You didn't leave the throne room; You're still seated on the throne!

Day 14: Jesus' Oneness with the Father

Psalm: Psalm 110

Scripture reading: John 17

Memory verse: ". . . That they may all be one; even as Thou, Father, art in Me, and I in Thee, that they also may be in Us; that the world may believe that Thou didst send Me" (John 17:21, NAS).

Praise and worship song: "Arise, My Soul, Arise"

> The Father hears Him pray,
> His dear Anointed One;
> He cannot turn away
> The presence of His Son;
> His Spirit answers to the blood,
> And tells me I am born of God.

Praise prompter: Do you know any Christians who live in foreign countries—perhaps a missionary, a relative, or a former colleague from work? Write their names and countries below, and thank God that you are brothers and sisters with them.

*Thoughts:*_____
_____
_____
_____

Prayer: Thank You, Father, for making me one with You and with my brothers and sisters all over the world! Show me what it means to walk in unity with them.

Day 15: Jesus' Name

Psalm: Psalm 8

Scripture reading: Acts 4

Memory verse: "And they [the high priests] commanded them not to speak or teach at all in the name of Jesus. But Peter and John answered . . . , 'We cannot stop speaking what we have seen and heard' " (Acts 4:18–20, NAS).

Praise and worship song: "Here in Your Presence"

> Name above all names, exalted forever
> To Jesus our Savior, our lives we surrender
> Standing before You
> We love and adore You
> O Lord, there is none like You

Praise prompter: How many names of Jesus can you think of? Write them in the space below, and then worship God for the character that each of these names represents. Here are a few to get you started: Lamb of God, Prince of Peace, Lion of Judah.

*Thoughts:*_____
_____
_____
_____
_____

Prayer: O Lord, truly there is no one who compares with You! You are all-powerful, all-complete, and I worship You.

Day 16: Jesus' Plan for My Life

Psalm: Psalm 116

Scripture reading: Isaiah 55

Memory verse: "For as the heavens are higher than the earth, so are My ways higher than your ways, and My thoughts than your thoughts" (Isaiah 55:9, NAS).

Praise and worship song: "We Are an Offering"

> All that we have, all that we are
> All that we hope to be
> We give to You, we give to You
> Lord, use our voices, Lord, use our hands
> Lord, use our lives, they are Yours
> We are an offering, we are an offering

Praise prompter: Have you ever wondered why something happened the way it did, and only years later found out it was the hand of God working out His perfect plan for your life? Write the circumstances below.

*Thoughts:*_____

_____

_____

_____

_____

_____

Prayer: Lord, help me to trust You, to give You my voice and hands and life, and then not try to take them back again!

Day 17: Jesus, the Lamb

Psalm: Psalm 139

Scripture reading: Revelation 7

Memory verse: "These are the ones who come out of the great tribulation, and they have washed their robes and made them white in the blood of the Lamb" (Revelation 7:14, NAS).

Praise and worship song: "I Hear Angels"

> Holy, holy, God almighty
> Who was, who is, and is to come
> All the angels are crying holy
> To the Lamb who sits upon the throne
>
> Holy, holy, God almighty
> Who was, who is, and is to come
> All creation is bringing glory
> To the Lamb who sits upon the throne

Praise prompter: Look up the word *lamb* in a concordance. List two passages from the Old Testament and two from the New that refer to Jesus as the sacrificial Lamb.

*Thoughts:*_____

_____

_____

_____

_____

Prayer: Father, I join with the angels in singing, "Holy, holy, God almighty, who was, who is, and is to come!" You are the God of my past, present, and future.

Day 18: Jesus, My Warrior

Psalm: Psalm 120

Scripture reading: Isaiah 35

Memory verse: "Say to those with palpitating heart, 'Take courage, fear not. Behold, your God will come with vengeance; the recompense of God will come, but He will save you' " (Isaiah 35:4, NAS).

Praise and worship song: "A Mighty Fortress Is Our God"

> Did we in our own strength confide,
> Our striving would be losing;
> Were not the right Man on our side,
> The Man of God's own choosing:
> Dost ask who that may be?
> Christ Jesus, it is He;
> Lord Sabaoth, His name,
> From age to age the same,
> And He must win the battle.

Praise prompter: Write down all the areas in your life where you need to see Jesus go to war on your behalf today. Now praise Him that He leads you into battle, and one by one declare Him your mighty Warrior over each of the situations that you listed.

*Thoughts:*_____
_____
_____

Prayer: Lord, help me remember to fight not with my own strength, but with the weapons that You've given me.

Day 19: Jesus' Grace

Psalm: Psalm 84

Scripture reading: Ephesians 1

Memory verse: "For the Lord God is a sun and shield; the Lord gives grace and glory; no good thing does He withhold from those who walk uprightly" (Psalm 84:11, NAS).

Praise and worship song: "Only by Grace"

> Only by grace can we enter, only by grace can we stand
> Not by our human endeavor, but by the blood of the Lamb
> Lord, if You mark our transgressions, who would stand?
> But thanks to Your grace we are cleansed by the blood
>   of the Lamb

Praise prompter: Think about a time when you tried to walk "uprightly," as Psalm 84:11 says, in the midst of an unrighteous situation. How did God give you grace to do that?

*Thoughts:*_____

_____

_____

_____

_____

_____

_____

Prayer: Lord, sometimes it's so hard to be a light shining in the darkness. I need Your grace today, or the flame might go out.

Day 20: Jesus, My Anchor

Psalm: Psalm 107

Scripture reading: Hebrews 6

Memory verse: "This hope we have as an anchor of the soul, a hope both sure and steadfast and one which enters within the veil" (Hebrews 6:19, NAS).

Praise and worship song: "The Solid Rock"

> When darkness veils His lovely face
> I rest on His unchanging grace;
> In ev'ry high and stormy gale,
> My anchor holds within the veil.
> On Christ, the solid rock, I stand;
> All other ground is sinking sand,
> All other ground is sinking sand.

Praise prompter: Draw a symbol of a stormy situation that you are currently weathering. Now draw an anchor to represent Jesus. Thank Him because He will always stay secure in "ev'ry high and stormy gale."

*Thoughts:*_____
_____
_____
_____
_____

Prayer: Lord, even when the storm threatens to drown me, please be my anchor today.

Day 21: Jesus' Love

Psalm: Psalm 117

Scripture reading: 1 John 3

Memory verse: "We know love by this, that He laid down His life for us" (1 John 3:16, NAS).

Praise and worship song: "Boundless Love"

> We rejoice, we rejoice in the name of the Lord
> We rejoice in His love today
> By His love we can conquer and do anything
> We rejoice in His love today
> Boundless love, boundless love
> He has conquered all of death and the grave
> Boundless love, boundless love
> By His love our souls are saved

Praise prompter: There's an old saying that "love conquers all." Describe an instance when you saw God's love "conquer all."

*Thoughts:*_____

_____

_____

_____

_____

Prayer: Holy Spirit, help me never to forget my Lord's great love for me, and to share that love with others.

Resources

If you would like to learn more about praise and worship, these resource materials will be helpful to you. They are available through your local Christian bookstore.

Books

Advanced Worship Seminar Manual, edited by Gerrit Gustafson. Worship Seminars International, Sylmar, California.

Contemporary Christian Music: Where It Came From, What It Is, Where It's Going, Paul Baker. Crossway Books, Westchester, Illinois. 1985.

Elements of Worship, Judson Cornwall. Bridge Publishing, Inc., South Plainfield, New Jersey. 1985.

The Endless Song: Music and Worship in the Church, Kenneth W. Osbeck. Kregel Publications, Grand Rapids, Michigan. 1987.

Entering and Enjoying Worship, Bob Mumford. Manna Christian Outreach, Greensburg, Pennsylvania. 1975.

Exploring Worship: A Practical Guide to Praise and Worship, Bob Sorge. Trinity Media Press, Buffalo, New York. 1987.

The Gift of Music: Great Composers and Their Influence, Jane Stuart Smith and Betty Carlson. Crossway Books, Westchester, Illinois. 1987.

The Gospel of Music: A Key to Understanding a Major

157

Chord of Ministry, Myron Noble. Apostolic Faith Churches of God, Inc., Washington, D.C. 1986.

Graham Kendrick's Make Way Handbook. Kingsway Publications, Ltd., E. Sussex, England. 1988.

The Hallelujah Factor: An Adventure into the Principles and Practice of Praise, Jack R. Taylor. Broadman Press, Nashville, Tennessee. 1983.

Jubilate! Church Music in the Evangelical Tradition, Donald P. Hustad. Hope Publishing Company, Carol Stream, Illinois. 1981.

Learning to Worship As a Way of Life, Graham Kendrick. Bethany House Publishers, Minneapolis, Minnesota. 1984.

Let Us Draw Near, Judson Cornwall. Logos International, South Plainfield, New Jersey. 1977.

Let Us Praise, Judson Cornwall. Logos International, South Plainfield, New Jersey. 1973.

Let Us Worship, Judson Cornwall. Bridge Publishing, Inc., South Plainfield, New Jersey. 1983.

Music Ministry, Mike and Viv Hibbert. Scripture in Song, Lewiston, New York. 1982.

101 Hymn Stories: Inspiring, Factual Backgrounds and Experiences that Prompted the Writing of 101 Selected Favorite Hymns, Kenneth W. Osbeck. Kregel Publications, Grand Rapids, Michigan. 1982.

101 More Hymn Stories: Inspiring, Factual Backgrounds and Experiences that Prompted the Writing of 101 Selected Favorite Hymns, Kenneth W. Osbeck. Kregel Publications, Grand Rapids, Michigan. 1985.

The Orchestra in Worship, Frank Longino. Selah Music Ministries, Pensacola, Florida. 1987.

The Power of His Presence, Graham Truscott. Restoration Temple, San Diego, California.

The Power of Praise and Worship: Discover the Source of

Power; Receive Your Healing through Praise; Experience God's Miracle Power Today, Terry Law. Victory House, Inc., Tulsa, Oklahoma. 1985.

Praise! A Matter of Life and Breath: Praising God in the Psalms, Ronald Barclay Allen. Thomas Nelson Publishers, Nashville, Tennessee. 1980.

Praise and Worship: In Earth As It Is in Heaven, Anne Murchison. Word Books, Waco, Texas. 1981.

The Praise Life of Jesus, Olen Griffing. Shady Grove Church Publications, Grand Prairie, Texas. 1985.

The Praise of His Glory, Bob Mason. Church on the Rock, Carrollton, Texas. 1987.

Praise Releases Faith: Transforming Power for Your Life, Terry Law. Victory House Publishers, Tulsa, Oklahoma. 1987.

The Prophetic Song, LaMar Boschman. Revival Press, Bedford, Texas. 1986.

The Rebirth of Music, LaMar Boschman. Revival Press, Little Rock, Arkansas. 1980.

Yet Will I Praise Him, Terry and Shirley Law with David Hazard. Chosen Books, Old Tappan, New Jersey. 1987.

Worship Is a Verb, Robert E. Webber. Word Books, Waco, Texas. 1985.

Worship: The Missing Jewel of the Evangelical Church, A. W. Tozer. Christian Publications, Camp Hill, Pennsylvania. 1979.

Magazines and Publications

The Psalmist. Kent Henry Ministries, St. Louis, Missouri.

Praise and Worship Music Tapes and Songbooks

Integrity Music: Hosanna! Music and Songbooks; Instrumental Series; and Alleluia! Music. Integrity Music, P.O. Box 16801, Mobile, Alabama 36616.

Maranatha! Music: Praise series and songbooks. Maranatha! Music, P.O. Box 31050, Laguna Hills, California 92654.

Scripture in Song: Music and songbooks. Scripture in Song, P.O. Box 525, Lewistown, New York 14092.

Teaching Tapes

A Dwelling Place with God, Geof Jackson. 8-tape series. Geof Jackson Ministries, P.O. Box 55236, Tulsa, Oklahoma 74155-1236.

Heaven on Earth, Charles Simpson. 4-tape series (#C48P). Charles Simpson Ministries, P.O. Box Z, Mobile, Alabama 36616.

Let the Temple Be Filled with His Glory, Charles Simpson. Single tape (#CS111). Charles Simpson Ministries, P.O. Box Z, Mobile, Alabama 36616.

The Power of Thanksgiving, Praise, and Worship, Charles Simpson. Single tape (#C444), part of *Keys to Christian Conquest*, 4-tape series (#C44P). Charles Simpson Ministries, P.O. Box Z, Mobile, Alabama 36616.

Praise, Derek Prince. Single tape (#4081). Derek Prince Ministries, P.O. Box 300, Ft. Lauderdale, Florida 33302.

Praise and Worship As a Lifestyle, Kent Henry. Kent Henry Ministries, 9820 E. Watson Road, St. Louis, Missouri 63126.

Praise and Worship Forum, 1988 James Robison Bible Conference, by Chuck Girard, Bruce Leafblad, Bob Mason, Gregory Owens, J. Daniel Smith, and Angela Tarlton. James Robison Ministries, P.O. Box 18489, Fort Worth, Texas 76118-9983.

Praise, Angels, and Victory, Terry Law. 2-tape series

(#4257). Law Outreach Ministries, P.O. Box 3563, Tulsa, Oklahoma 74101.

The Sacrifice of Praise, Terry Law. 2-tape series (#4258). Law Outreach Ministries, P.O. Box 3563, Tulsa, Oklahoma 74101.

Worship Seminar, John Wimber and Carl Tuttle. Vineyard Ministries International, P.O. Box 65004, Anaheim, California 92805.

Special Service for Churches

Christian Copyright Licensing, Inc. (CCLI) CCLI offers churches a convenient, affordable and legal way to duplicate copyrighted songs for congregational use (e.g., in bulletins or on overhead transparencies). By purchasing a single annual license, churches have access to more than 100,000 songs from 225 publishers (including Integrity Music). Contact CCLI, 7031 N.E. Halsey St., Portland, OR 97213; (800) 234-2446 or (503) 257-2230.